Praise for *The First Two Rules of Leadership*

"Leading this way will result in an engaged, inspired, and highly productive team while also being more fun and fulfilling for the leader."

—Kip Tindell, Co-Founder and Chairman, The Container Store (one of *Fortune*'s top 100 places to work for 14 years in a row)

"Simple, practical, and profound rules to help you become a great leader. A must read for any leader."

—Lorraine Grubbs, former Director of Employment, Southwest Airlines

"David Cottrell's latest book is a must read for any leader. It simplifies the complexity of leadership into two simple rules. Read, then implement and get ready for sustained leadership success."

—Pat Williams, Senior Vice President of the Orlando Magic; author of *The Success Intersection*

"This book simplifies the complexities of leadership and helps leaders lead with clarity, integrity, and focus."

—Jon Gordon, author of *The Energy Bus* and *The Carpenter*

"David Cottrell shares valuable insights on how to be the leader others will strive to emulate. With acumen and sincerity, *The First Two Rules of Leadership* succinctly lays out a sustained methodology for hiring smart, coaching performance, and leading with poise."

—Kimberly Rath, President, Talent Plus, Inc. (recognized as an Achievers 50 Most Engaged Workplace)

"Two simple rules of leadership that will improve your effectiveness as a leader. . . ."

—T. Michael Glenn, Executive Vice President, FedEx

"This book simplifies the complexities of leadership down to two logical, necessary rules: Make smarter decisions and lead with class."

—Karl Koch, Vice President and General Manager, Enterprise Holdings

HOW TO ACHIEVE EXTRAORDINARY RESULTS WITH CLASS

the First
Two Rules
of
Leadership

☑ Don't be Stupid
☑ Don't be a Jerk

David Cottrell

Bestselling Author of The *Monday Morning* Series

WILEY

For general information about our other products and services, please contact our Customer Care Department within the United States at (800) 762-2974, outside the United States at (317) 572-3993 or fax (317) 572-4002.

Wiley publishes in a variety of print and electronic formats and by print-on-demand. Some material included with standard print versions of this book may not be included in e-books or in print-on-demand. If this book refers to media such as a CD or DVD that is not included in the version you purchased, you may download this material at http://booksupport.wiley.com. For more information about Wiley products, visit www.wiley.com.

ISBN 9781119282808 (cloth); ISBN 9781119282822 (ebk);
ISBN 9781119282952 (ebk)

Printed in the United States of America.

10   9   8   7   6   5   4   3   2   1

Contents

Introduction

Every day thousands of people quit their jobs. They reach their limit and realize that enough is enough. They bid farewell to friends and co-workers. They exit a familiar, comfortable place and enter an unknown territory—new job, boss, peers, and environment. They are convinced that the unknown has got to be better than the current situation that they know all too well. They believe that anything, anywhere, would be better than where they are.

So, they leave.

During their last day on the job, they have an exit interview with human resources and are asked: "Why are you leaving?" They respond that they will be paid more at the new job, the benefits are better, the new job is closer to home, or the hours are better.

In most cases, this is not the whole picture.

If you believe the exit interviews, great people leave good organizations to start over someplace else because of money or for more advancement opportunities. Why would they say anything else? After all, the person leaving doesn't want to burn any bridges and has nothing to gain by telling the whole truth. Instead, they give reasons that are believable, but not accurate. Most exit interviews do not uncover the whole truth.

Occasionally, the difference in money is significant enough to warrant a move, but most of the time it's not about money or career advancement. Money is only one piece of the puzzle, and perhaps a small one at that. Most people want more than just a paycheck—they want to feel good about where they work, who they work with, and what they accomplish together as a team. In one survey, 89 percent of leaders stated that they believed employees leave because of money.[1] Yet in a parallel survey of employees who left organizations, 88 percent of people said they left for reasons not related to money.[2] Let those statistics sink in . . . only 12 percent of people left because of money. In another recent study of 17,000 people, less than 10 percent cited compensation and advancement opportunities as the most critical aspects of a job.[3]

Consider the situation from the perspective of the interviewer: When *you* interview someone for a position and ask them why they are considering leaving their current job, what do they say? Have you ever heard anyone say, "Because you are going to pay me more"? Probably not. The most common response is something like, "Because my efforts and contributions aren't appreciated where I'm currently working." If people on your team are interviewing with other organizations, that is probably the same answer they are giving in their interviews.

People who plan to leave do not want to initiate a confrontation. They just want to walk out the door and not look back. They want to escape from a situation that has become toxic to them. Most have reached a point where they hate coming to work.

Even more problematic is when you have people on your team who are disengaged. They have mentally resigned from their job—and have told everyone but you that they are "out of here." Those employees will do far more damage to your team's performance than anything a competitor could do. They infiltrate your team with disloyalty, distrust, and apathy.

The truth is that most people who quit and leave, or those who quit and stay, made a decision to quit their leader. Their resignation or disengagement has little to do with pay, benefits, distance from home, or long hours. They quit because something between them and their leader has gone awry. The desire and ability to do a good job became overshadowed by the obstacles and frustrations faced every day. Ironically, most of those frustrations were created by the very person who, on the first day at their new job, enthusiastically greeted them, shook their hand, and welcomed them as an important link on the team.

Of course, some people quit simply because they are not in the right job for them at this time in their life. But these people are rare exceptions rather than the rule.

Do people quit because their leader is incompetent? Probably not. Most leaders are in the roles they are in because they have the competency to do the job well. Do they quit because of the leader's lack of desire? It's probably not that either. Most leaders want to do a good job and want be successful.

People quit because they are exhausted. They are exhausted from implementing bad decisions. They are exhausted from redoing work when decisions were made before all the facts were considered. They are exhausted because they perceive that their leader's ego is preventing the nourishment of a positive work environment. They are exhausted from trying to figure out why incredibly smart people keep asking them to implement decisions that appear to be really dumb. They are exhausted from working for leaders who they think really do not care about them.

They are exhausted because their leaders are not empowering them or supporting them, and they are thus prevented from doing their best work. They lose trust in the person who is supposed to be leading them and they start looking for someone else they can trust.

Long-term effective leaders are competent and also passionate, trustworthy, creative, and humane. The Gallup organization found that the single most important variable in employee productivity is the quality of the relationship between employees and their direct supervisors.[4] That relationship requires a leader whose expectations are reasonable, is consistent, cares about them, values their uniqueness, and encourages their growth and development.

Great leaders develop skills that help them understand people and get results through the efforts of other people. Leadership is complex because you are dealing with real people, each of whom has needs and desires. The greatest leaders learn how to break the complex task of dealing positively with everyone on their team into its simplest form.

The First Two Rules of Leadership is direct and simple. It is not about a new leadership strategy. Strategies come and go. What you will learn in this book is tried and true regardless of the strategic focus of the time. Likewise, the principles apply to businesses in every industry, as well as schools, hospitals, churches, and even homes.

If you are a leader who wants to improve morale on your team, decrease turnover, increase your own job satisfaction, improve results, and have a whole lot more fun leading, this book is for you. Regardless of your current situation or how you got to where you are, the next move is yours. This book outlines how you can make better decisions and treat your team with dignity and respect at the same time.

The people on your team want to win and they want to be led by a winner. You are that leader. Read, pay attention, and follow the first two rules for leaders: Don't be stupid and don't be a jerk.

DON'T BE STUPID

"Our budget is tight. Let's change the team-building exercise we have planned into a self-help study course."
—Action item from a leadership strategy session

No one is calling *you* stupid. Actually, stupid is the opposite of what you are. You are probably one of the smartest people in any room you enter. You are likely well educated, experienced, and qualified to become a great leader. You are respected and your team really wants to help you succeed.

But, sometimes your team is asked to do things that seem to them, quite frankly, stupid. Of course it is not intentional, so maybe you could eliminate some choices that wind up making them look foolish.

Every leader gets caught up in the pressure of the moment and does things that—upon reflection—were pretty stupid. Dumb things like: hiring in haste, rewarding actions that work against what you are really trying to accomplish, not paying attention to the needs of your team, or piling on more work and leading your superstars directly to burnout and checkout.

The first section of the book will address areas where many have looked stupid in the past and provide some suggestions to make smarter decisions in the future.

You can become the leader you want to be! Make smarter choices and win with class, beginning right now.

Don't Be Stupid
Hire Smart

"Here we go again. Another new person. Why did he hire this person? Everybody knows he won't last. This is stupid."

"I am not going to spend my time helping another rookie. He is on his own."

—Conversation between two tenured employees

Meets minimum qualifications? Check.
References? Check.
Background check? Check.
Drug test? Check.
Decent interview? Check.
Hire? Not so fast, my friend.

Smart hiring is not easy hiring. Smart hiring is hiring tough.

If the best opportunity to improve a team's performance is to hire smart, why do people hire quickly and in a vacuum to fill an open position? That is pretty stupid. You never really know what you are getting until the new person is already on the team, but you can increase your chances of getting a great person if you hire smart.

The most valuable asset in your organization is having the right people on your team; everyone knows that. However, some people tend to ignore the fact that the greatest liability any team faces is having the wrong people on your team. You cannot have a strong and effective team with weak and ineffective people. In fact, there is nothing any competitor can do to hurt your team as much as your hiring the wrong person to be on your team.

Hiring easy is welcoming the first person who barely meets the minimum qualifications of your team. That sounds fine, but it is stupid to hire easy. If you hire tough, your job will be easier; if you hire easy, your job will be a lot tougher. It should be a privilege for someone to earn his or her way on to your team.

Even if your team has to cover an open position, which involves extra work for a while, they want you to hire tough. They do not want to cover for an easy hire who will drag the entire team down with them. No one wants you to hire tough more than the people already on your team.

Granted, you have a lot on your plate and hiring is just one of the many tasks you are responsible for overseeing. And, whether you admit it or not, you are probably not a great interviewer. Don't take that personally; it's not a poor reflection on you. It is simply because you do not hire a lot of people and you do not use your interviewing skills very often. If you hire only a few people a year, you are not going to be a great interviewer. But you can have a great interview process.

Smart Hiring

The major reason for stupid hiring is lack of preparation. To hire smart, you have to prepare smart. It is not smart to begin preparing for the interview when the candidate is waiting in your lobby. How can you make a great decision if you are not adequately prepared for what you want to decide on?

Failing to prepare—winging it—is no way to treat someone who will become either your most valuable asset or your most costly liability. Instead, clearly and accurately define, in writing, the skills and attributes the perfect candidate will bring to your organization. Then, prepare every question—and your ideal answer—in advance so that you spend your time listening and evaluating rather than trying to figure out what question to ask next. Creating an interview outline will help keep you on track. Ask each candidate the same questions in the same order so you can concentrate on and evaluate their responses.

Another issue associated with stupid hiring is that you are emotionally involved. The open position is taking time and energy away from you, so you want to fill the job fast. The leader makes a subjective decision based on personality rather than an objective decision based on fact. Your emotions want the person to "fit," even though they may not be the *right* fit. You will be far better off if you take your time and find the right person. Get someone in HR or a peer to help—they're not faced with the same emotions you have about your openings.

Following these three rules of three will help you hire smart:

1. Interview at least three qualified candidates for every position.
2. Interview the candidates three times.
3. Have three people evaluate the candidates.

Interviewing at least three qualified candidates for every position sounds like a long process, and it is. But to hire tough and get the right person on your team, you need to have choices. If there is only one qualified person you are evaluating, you do not have a choice. Find three qualified people and make a smart choice on who would fit best with your team.

When you interview someone three times, you can make a smarter decision. Schedule the interviews at varying times of the day. If your initial interview was in the morning, interview the candidate the next time in the afternoon or evening. You'll be working with them all day, so why not see what they're like at different times of the day?

When evaluating candidates, consider talent and fit equally. The most talented person may not be the best choice if they don't fit with the talent that already exists on your team. The best information regarding fit will come from the superstars on your team, so it is smart to involve them in the process. They know the job and the culture and will have a good feel for whether the candidate will be a good fit on your team. Most of your top performers will look on their involvement as a reward and take ownership of the success of the person you hire. They will probably help in their orientation and do what they can to help them to be successful. That is a good deal for everyone. If some of your superstars are not interested in helping in the interview process, don't force them to do it. But if they are interested in helping, they are a great source of information.

Seeing Their Best

If you hire smart, you won't "stretch" a candidate into being the person that you want them to be. If the job you are seeking to fill has been open for a while, it is natural for you to hear what you want to hear, see what you want to see, and convince yourself that you will coach the candidate to become the perfect employee—the exact awesome individual you need. Be careful; when a position that you are responsible for has been open for an extended period of time, you are vulnerable. Your stress builds and you pressure yourself. My experience has been that the longer a position is open, the better the next candidate looks. Before long, anyone who can fog a mirror is the perfect, obvious choice for your opening. Smart hiring does not work that way. If you hire candidates that are "on the fence" simply to get the job filled, you will pay the consequences later.

What you see in the candidate during the interview will not get significantly better once they are hired. Oh, they will develop more experience, but you are seeing them at their very best. During the interview, their smiles are the brightest, attitudes are can-do, personal hygiene is flawless, working hours are not an issue, and they are willing to do whatever you want them to do. When they are hired, things tend to change—at least a little.

Slow down the hiring process and hire smart. Don't hesitate to hire someone who you may perceive as being smarter than you—that person will help everyone on your team become better.

Your team wants to work with people who show a desire to work, have a talent for doing the job, and exhibit values that fit with your corporate values. You can be the greatest leader in the world, but if you have people on your team who are not talented, you will not be successful. Hiring a warm body just to fill a position means a lot more work for everyone on your team.

Southwest Airlines follows the philosophy that it's best to "hire attitude, train skill." Of course there are limitations—you would not want to hire a charismatic person to be a pilot if she can't fly a plane. But, if one applicant meets the minimum qualifications and has a great attitude about work and life, and another applicant has a little more experience and slightly less enthusiasm, Southwest would hire the less experienced person. Southwest believes that skills can be trained, a good attitude cannot.

The Container Store describes their hire-tough philosophy as 1=3. They believe one great hire is equivalent to three good hires. In fact, they pay their associates almost double the average pay for the same job and have proven that 1=3 yields a great return on their hire-tough investment.

If you hire the best people and effectively train and coach them, you won't have to hire very many. Having great people on the team is less stressful and more enjoyable for everyone. And being around great people makes you better.

It is not smart to go to all the trouble of hiring a great person and then expecting them to immediately fit right into your environment. Start them off right. Your onboarding process should go well beyond a human resources orientation and assigning a mentor. Answer the questions every new employee wants to know: What is my role? What are your expectations? How do I fit into the big picture? How does my job matter? Answer those four questions up front and you have a good chance to watch that person grow into a great employee.

You will only be a great leader if you have great people. If a candidate's very best still leaves you "on the fence" as to whether they are the right candidate, it would be stupid to hire them. Keep looking! Never lower your standards just to fill a position! You and your team will all pay for it later.

Don't be stupid. Hire smart.

Don't Be Stupid
Coach Smart

"My superstars don't need to be coached. I just need to stay out of their way."

—The leader

"I never received any encouragement. It was like I was being ignored."

—A superstar who resigned

Cornell University psychology professors David Dunning and Justin Kruger conducted a groundbreaking study in 1999 evaluating how people viewed their own performance. The study, now known as the Dunning–Kruger Effect, concluded that people base their perceptions of performance, in part, on their preconceived notions about their skills. Often those judgments about their performance have little to do with their actual accomplishment. Most people see their performance the way they want to see it. Lower-level performers viewed their performance as much greater than their actual performance. Top performers were typically more critical of their performance and underestimated the impact they had on their success and those around them. In both cases, the study concluded that people see themselves differently than reality and neither group is great at improving what they don't know.[1]

Everybody needs a coach! No one on your team can be objective when it comes to his or her performance. Even your superstars need someone who has a different perspective and can suggest minor adjustments that yield better results. You can give better advice than the person can come up with on their own. They may not want or need you telling them exactly what to do and how to do it. After all, they were hired and trained to do their job. But they also do not want to be unnoticed. The fact is that many great people go to bed hungry at night—hungry for encouragement and recognition from leaders. Even though they may not admit it, they need and want to be coached.

The root meaning of the verb "to coach" is to bring a person from where they are to where they want to be. It is your responsibility to provide every person on your team with guidance to help them get where they want to be. If they are doing things right, then reinforce that behavior. If they have gotten off course, let them know what they need to change in order to improve. You are the coach.

Myths of Coaching

There are a few myths about coaching that need to be debunked up front. The first is that people do not want to be held accountable. Your best performers do want to be held accountable—that's part of the reason why they are the best. Your lowest performers probably will not be keen on the idea. But in the end, everyone wants everyone else to be held accountable. Without accountability and guidance, you will never be able to move your team forward.

The second myth is that coaching is solely about working with your lowest performers. Not true. If you are spending the majority of your time with your lowest performers, you will drive yourself crazy. Don't be stupid. Spend time with your best performers, too. They will build you up and let you clearly see how things can be better.

Another common misconception is that silence on your part sends a signal that your team is doing just fine (as in, if they weren't doing well, you'd be sure to let them know). Your silence is loud and it communicates to people, but it may not be sending the message you intend to send. Every person on your team needs your guidance to know how they are doing.

The final coaching myth is that by fulfilling your organization's formal performance reviews every six months or once a year, you have sufficiently coached and provided feedback to your team. That would be like a football coach only coaching when the season is half over. Sounds sort of stupid, doesn't it? But that is what you are doing if you provide feedback and guidance only at review time.

Formal reviews rarely change long-term behavior. An employee's behavior may change a few weeks before the review—as in, "I want my manager to have a fresh memory of the good things I'm doing." And behavior change may last a few weeks after the session ("I did pay attention to my manager's guidance"). But, in general, what little coaching happens during performance reviews isn't effective. Seldom will it last until the next performance review. Many organizations have recently abolished the performance review. Long-term behavior change occurs only if you, like any effective coach, consistently provide feedback and guidance.

Everyone Is Not the Same

In a perfect world every member of a team would have the desire and talent to be the very best at their job. The right person would always be doing the right job—wouldn't that be great? But, in reality, it seldom happens that everyone is pulling an equal share of the load.

Most teams are composed of three performance groups— superstars, sometimes stars, and sleeping stars.

Superstars

The superstars are the people on your team who have the experience, knowledge, commitment, and desire to be the very best at their jobs. A superstar is the right person in the right job. You know who they are—they are obvious for all to see. The superstars typically comprise 10 to 20 percent of your team and are the ones you can depend on to do everything required before they are even asked. They are dependable, trustworthy, and the very best at their job.

Some leaders think superstars shouldn't be bothered with coaching. They think that superstars prefer to work independently and deserve to be left alone. That is normally not the case. While superstars may not want or need you telling them what to do and how to do it, they also don't want to be ignored. Superstars are often people with strong personalities and egos who need to be appreciated—but most of the time they will not say they need any attention. Don't be fooled. If you ignore them, they may think that you don't care about them and start looking for somebody who does care.

It is stupid to ignore your superstars. Instead you should pay special attention to them.

You would like a larger percentage of your team to be superstars, but often your best players are promoted to additional responsibilities, which is a good thing. However, some superstars leave because the leader inadvertently punishes them for being a superstar by piling more work on them. To compensate for underperformers, top performers are loaded up with extra work. You don't intend to punish the superstar, yet that is exactly what can happen. That's stupid. Don't abuse your superstars and take away the incentives for them to keep working at the superstar level. Once they see that mediocrity gets rewarded, their performance may decline, which is exactly the opposite of what you want. Your job is not to lower the bar by adjusting for and accommodating the lowest-performing employees. You should be raising that bar by recognizing and rewarding superstar behaviors.

But don't micromanage your superstars, either. They know what to do—that is why they are superstars. Here are a few tips to help keep your superstars motivated:

1. Give them the freedom to get the job done. Freedom is not ignoring them. It is demonstrating confidence in them by allowing autonomy but also paying attention and providing active, positive feedback and guidance.
2. Allow them the opportunity to stretch their thinking by asking their opinion of issues outside their typical job. When you ask for their expertise, you build self-esteem.

3. Recognize their outstanding work publicly. Don't be scarce with superstar compliments.

4. Encourage them to teach and coach other superstars. It is natural to want them to work with your lower performers but your superstars can learn from each other, encourage each other, and figure out ways to do their job even better.

5. Ask your superstar to mentor a new employee. It will build their self-esteem and bring the new person up to speed faster on how to get results within your organization. Those who teach also learn more—a win-win for all.

Sometimes Stars

The second group—normally about half of any team—are the sometimes stars. They may not have the experience to be a superstar yet. Or maybe they are former superstars who, for some reason, lost their motivation to be the best. They could be your superstars of the future, or they could fall backward.

The sometimes stars are "on the bubble" contributors. Some days they exceed your expectations and on other days they fall a bit short. Making up the largest portion of your team, the sometimes stars are also the backbone. They have the potential to be superstars—or sleeping stars. Your ability to coach and positively affect the performance of this group is critical to your success.

Often, it's the small things you do that inspire the sometimes stars to become superstars—things like remembering facts about them and their family, asking their opinions, taking the time to listen, or merely doing something special when they need a boost. To raise the performance bar on your team, you have to have your sometimes stars moving up to superstar status.

Sometimes stars are your leverage for improvement. They have their eyes wide open and are watching you constantly. They are evaluating how you treat the superstars and then they make the decision whether to pay the price to be a superstar, hang in the sometime star land, or do even less.

Here are some tips to help your sometimes stars become superstars:

1. Treat your superstars like superstars. The most important thing you can do is to make it obvious that the price your employee will have to pay to become a superstar is worthwhile.
2. Be candid. Specifically explain what they can do to become a superstar. Identify an action plan and help them get to where they want to be.
3. Spend time with them so that you can know specifically how to coach them to improve their performance. The more information you have, the better you can provide them a path to becoming a superstar.
4. Provide them an opportunity to improve their skills. They can analyze trends, make a presentation, attend a seminar, or represent your team at a function. Allow them to be a little uncomfortable as they work to improve their skills.

Sleeping Stars

Finally, there are the sleeping stars. Those are the ones who are doing as little as they can get away with. They consistently fail to carry their share of the load. In fact, not only are they not doing their own jobs, but there's also a good chance that they're preventing the superstars from doing their jobs as well. This is a group that must be managed or dealt with if you want to be successful.

A sleeping star who is not right for the job and who creates a negative environment within the work group will destroy your team. They have more influence on your team than any competitor could. If you refuse to address the problem of an incompetent employee, it may be time to reevaluate just who is incompetent . . . or who's not doing their job.

If you are like most, you think that the minimum level of expected performance should be in the sometimes-star group. However, look around. Sleeping stars are still on your team, which indicates that their performance is acceptable to you. In fact, many leaders actually reward their sleeping stars by giving them less work, fewer expectations, acknowledgment with a decent performance review, and a pay raise at the end of the year.

That is stupid.

When you do that, you should expect more people to fall into the sleeping-star category. It's not rocket science that when people figure out they can do less and still get rewarded, they will do less. That would be in most people's nature, unfortunately.

Are You Coaching Smart?

Try this exercise: Write down the name of each team member and then categorize them as superstars, sometimes stars, or sleeping stars. You know exactly into which group every person on your team fits.

Then, check your files, retrieve every person's most recent performance review, and put their most recent performance review score next to their name. Next, pull their personnel file. Beside each name, note each time that you've documented some kind of recognition or performance improvement over the past six months. It could be a letter of appreciation or a performance improvement document.

Now, answer the questions: Are your superstars being rewarded? Are your sometimes stars being challenged to become superstars? Do your sleeping stars know where they stand? You may discover that there is little difference between how the top performers and the lowest performers are treated. The issue may not be an employee issue. It could be a leadership issue of not recognizing and rewarding the behaviors you want.

You simply cannot hide in management land, ignore performance issues, and expect your superstars to stick around for very long.

Don't be stupid. Coach smart.

Don't Be Stupid
Deal with the Sleeping Stars

"I am sick and tired of redoing and covering up what he messed up. Why doesn't she see that he is killing us?"

—A sometimes star complaining to a superstar

I hope no one told you that leadership would be easy. It is not.

Many leaders think that they can turn the poor performance of every one of their sleeping stars around by providing them with superb guidance. That is your first objective—to coach and guide them to a better performance level. There are some sleeping stars that you can help wake up and guide to become sometimes stars and even eventually superstars.

But, many times a person is in the wrong job for them and they can't help it. If that is the case, you have to make a decision about how much time, energy, and effort you are going to invest in the turnaround. I don't want to discourage you from giving every effort to turn the employee around, but if you have done everything you can do and there is no improvement, there may be a greater reason for their lack of performance: They are not the right person for your particular job. At that point, even Vince Lombardi could not turn them around. It is time for you to deal with the bigger issue.

Leadership Lesson from the Links

I love to play golf and I think there are hundreds of leadership lessons that can be learned from the great game of golf. One of the lessons is to make sure you have the right equipment to be successful.

Not too long ago, I bought a new golf club—a driver—that was going be the answer to my game. It had the latest technology, was made of the newest materials, and looked great. The golf magazines gave this club the highest ratings and I was really proud of my new club—until I started hitting balls with it. I hit hundreds of balls on the driving range and on the course. The ball just would not go where I wanted it to go. You can imagine my frustration.

Finally, after investing several hundreds of dollars in that driver, along with hours of practice and many bad shots on the course, I had to make a decision. What was I going to do with this club?

One alternative was to leave the driver in the bag and try to fool myself into thinking I had not made a mistake. The problem with the "ignore it" strategy was that I still needed a driver. The rules of golf allow me to carry only 14 clubs, so keeping a club that didn't work for me would prevent me from getting another club that I would trust and could hit consistently. Ignoring the problem was not a good choice.

Another alternative was to keep using the driver. Even after hundreds of bad hits, my pride was telling me that I was good enough to work it out. I continued using the driver and was again punished with slices, hooks, rough, trees, sand, and out-of-bounds shots. Hitting with this club was driving me crazy, hurting my game, killing my confidence, and affecting my attitude. If the rest of my clubs could talk, they probably would say that they didn't like it either because I had to hit with them instead of my new, fancy driver. Continuing to use the club was stupid.

The alternative I chose was to accept the fact this club was not right for me. Although it came highly recommended and was a great club for other golfers, it was not the right club for my game, even though I had invested so much of my time, attention, and energy to make it work. Ultimately, I chose to accept the financial loss and the loss of pride, and sold that driver to someone more suited for it. My friend who bought it from me became a better golfer with the same club that was hurting my attitude, patience, ego, and score.

Now that I have another driver in my bag, I can hit well, and feel confident hitting. The problem was not my swing or my club. The problem was that my swing was not right for that particular club. Once I accepted the fact that I had done everything I could with the expensive, high-tech, good-looking club that did not work for me, I was able to improve my game.

The same lesson applies in leadership. People who are not the best fit for the position on your team may be an exact fit for someone else's position. The faster you act after making a decision to de-hire, the better it is for you and your team.

Your Toughest Job

The impact of having an incompetent employee on your team will not disappear by itself. When sleeping stars figure out they can do less and still get rewarded, they'll continue to do just that. There's no reason to do more. And while you're giving them their second or third "one more chance," they could be destroying your team. The next move is yours.

Letting someone go is one of the toughest tasks leaders face. Although problem employees represent a small percentage of your team, they take up a disproportionate amount of your time, energy, and enthusiasm—all of which could be used in more constructive ways. De-hiring someone is emotional, and many times the policies of your organization make it even more difficult. You may rationalize that it takes too long and you are not sure it is worth the trouble.

Whether or not you know it, your team is depending on you to deal with the sleeping star. The single greatest demotivator of a team is to have people around who are sapping energy and not carrying their share of the load. Keeping sleeping stars on your team is like having four batteries in a remote control and one of them is dead. Before long, the bad battery will zap all of the energy from the good batteries and the remote will not work at all. At that point, it is difficult to even know which battery began as the bad one. That is what sleeping stars who are in the wrong job do—they drag down all those around them and eventually your team's progress will come to a screeching halt.

It takes courage to address issues honestly and then let people go when that's the action you need to take. You have a lot at stake. Your emotions are involved, the employee's short-term livelihood is involved, it is a tough conversation to have, and your team is watching. But, if you have provided someone every opportunity for success and his performance still fails to meet expectations, summon your courage and address the situation. It is not a personal mistake of yours, nor is it the employee's mistake—the job is just not right for him.

It is stupid not to deal with the sleeping stars quickly, decisively, and fairly.

Check Yourself

Before you begin the process of terminating someone, check yourself. Here are seven questions to answer so you can be confident that you have done everything possible to address the situation:

1. Have I made my expectations crystal clear? Specifically, where is the gap in my expectations and his results?
2. Are my expectations reasonable and fair?
3. Have they received adequate training to do the job properly?
4. Do they understand why it's important to do the job correctly?
5. Am I holding them accountable for their performance? Are there appropriate and consistent consequences for nonperformance?
6. Have I given them the freedom to be successful?
7. Have all performance obstacles been removed?

Be honest in your evaluation. If you have given responsibility without resources, the person you hire as a replacement will probably generate the same results. It is stupid to demand responsibility without providing resources.

If you can truthfully answer yes to all seven of those questions, you have done your job. The issue lies with the employee. Don't allow yourself to be seduced by the sleeping star's potential or your pride. Tell the truth: The job is just not right for them.

The process of de-hiring someone is challenging at best. But, believe it or not, it is good that it is tough to de-hire people. Stringent rules are in place to make sure you are fair and consistent, not to prevent you from letting someone go who cannot do the job. The experts in human resources are there to help you through the process if you have done your job in establishing your code of conduct, providing feedback, and holding them accountable. What drives human resources crazy is when a leader wants to de-hire someone who, a few months ago, received a great performance review. I have seen that time and time again. The leader blames HR for making it too tough to let go of someone that they recently gave a good performance review. That is not HR's fault.

In the short term, letting someone go is painful. It is terrible. No one enjoys the experience. You are placed in an unfamiliar and unwanted position. Regardless of the circumstances that led to the termination, your role is to maintain their dignity and deal with it as compassionately as possible. There is no way you can know exactly how they will react when you have to deliver the news. The day of termination could be the worst day of that person's life. Losing a job is not just about the loss of pay or a position; it is also about losing a community of friends. Do the best you can to offer assistance and empathy. They may take their frustration out on you—that is a natural reaction—don't fight back. Your role is to protect their dignity in any way possible. Everyone will be evaluating how you handle this difficult part of your job. The people remaining on your team are watching. The person who is de-hired will remember how you treated them. Do your best to make sure that everyone sees that you handled the situation respectfully, regardless of how the employee accepted the news.

However, in the long term, it is your job to improve your team, and there is a price associated with keeping sleeping stars on the team. Coach them and give them plenty of time to come around, but after you have done all you can do, you need to move forward.

The Irony

My experience has been that most of the de-hired employees will eventually attest that it was the best thing that ever happened to them. As unbelievable as that may sound, many times an unwanted termination forces someone to move from a job that isn't right for them to something more aligned with their talents and interests. It forces them to take their future into their own hands. Their best is yet to come, but it requires being in a job that's a better fit for them. With few exceptions, it's also the best thing for the remainder of the team . . . and you.

Steve Jobs was de-hired from Apple. He had led the company to profitability and success but at 30 years old he was let go. Years later, through a series of unusual and remarkable events, he was reinstated as CEO of Apple.

Here is what he said about getting fired: "I didn't see it then, but it turned out that getting fired from Apple was the best thing that could have ever happened to me. The heaviness of being successful was replaced by the lightness of being a beginner again, less sure about everything. It freed me to enter one of the most creative periods of my life."[1]

You can probably name several people who were let go and then found their "right job." But at the time they were de-hired, they certainly didn't see it that way. They were probably bitter, frustrated, and angry at management. It was management's fault. That anger and frustration should be expected.

In the short term they will blame you. If they were in the wrong job for them and you forced them to find the right job for them, you did the right thing.

Don't be stupid. Protect your team and deal with sleeping stars with respect, dignity, and speed.

Don't Be Stupid
Synchronize

"We know that communication is a problem, but we are not going to discuss it with our employees."

—Overheard at a leadership conference

Synchronized swimming has been an Olympic sport since 1984. It's beautiful to watch but very demanding for swimmers, requiring fitness, stamina, and flexibility. It is amazing to see how a team is able to perform perfectly in sync while they are both upside down and underwater—especially when you consider that the only equipment allowed in synchronized swimming is a nose plug.

Olympic-caliber synchronized swim teams must work in perfect unison. It would be stupid to allow everyone to do their own thing. Every person must know their individual role, when to perform each move, and how each of them affects the team's performance. When every swimmer is in sync, the performance is breathtaking. But if even one team member is out of sync at any point, the entire performance falls apart—the whole team looks uncoordinated and out of rhythm.

The same is true with your team. Synchronization around what is *really* important is absolutely critical for your success. The military refers to this synchronization as "unity of effort"—harmonizing the efforts of different people toward a common goal. When every individual on your team clearly understands what is really important and each person is unified in working toward those goals, your performance can be spectacular and profitable. But without unification people do their own thing and lose focus. Before you know it, forward movement comes to a halt and any chance of achieving the team's targets or completing tasks can be lost.

Why Synchronize?

In survey after survey, year after year, inconsistent and confusing internal communication is identified as the greatest frustration felt by employees in almost every organization. What a team is asked to do and what they are held accountable for is out of sync with the priorities of the organization. How could that be?

If you are like most leaders, you spend so much time and effort communicating, it's hard to believe synchronization could be a major problem. A common leadership paradox is that while employees are frustrated by a perceived lack of communication, most leaders feel they are world-class communicators. In one study,[1] researchers asked a group of leaders to evaluate their personal communication skills. The study revealed that 90 percent of leaders rate their communication skills in the top 10 percent of all leaders. Obviously, 80 percent of the leaders think they are better communicators than their followers perceive them to be. That is quite a gap from world class.

The reality is that, no matter the industry or size of the organization you are in, you work in a constant state of change that, unfortunately, creates synchronization static. As a result, team members become frustrated, thinking, "We are out of the loop. . . . Things are always changing. . . . I don't know what they want. . . . I'm not a mind reader. . . . The target is always moving. . . . It's hard to figure out what to focus on."

You are likely frustrated, too. Reading this, are you thinking, "Are you kidding me? Communication is not our problem." You may think that the individuals on your team should be totally synchronized around what you are trying to accomplish together. After all, you have clearly defined mission statements, job descriptions, performance reviews, emails, memos, texts, motivational posters, screen savers, and myriad other ways of communicating what is really important. They just don't listen.

It is possible that both sides are right.

Communication may not be the problem, and communicating more may not be the solution. In most cases, people do not need more information. Much of the information they receive doesn't get read; what they do read is frequently misunderstood; and what they do understand is easily forgotten. That's not a knock on your team. It's just that there is so much communicating going on that it is difficult to determine what information is really important out of all the stuff that is not so important. So rather than communicating more, you need to be synchronizing.

Whether you like it or not, the person receiving your communication decides whether that communication successfully conveys the necessary information. Effective, synchronized communication is not about you—it's about them. It's not about the message that gets transmitted—it's about the message that gets received. But you can help synchronize by transmitting each message accurately, consistently, simply, and effectively.

Synchronization is not easy. You may be saying and writing the right things but:

- What they hear is what counts, not what you say. And, unfortunately many times they hear what they want to hear. A two-way process is essential to communication synchronization. Every employee may have a different interpretation of what you say. Without feedback from your team and constant and consistent reinforcement from you to make sure they understand completely what you are communicating, your team will be out of sync.

- What they read is what counts, not what you write. Email and text messaging are great communication tools for some things. However, no one can read your mind, tone, or inflection. Consider the following statement and as you read it, emphasize the words that are underlined:
  - *I never said you stole the money.*
  - <u>I</u> never said you stole the money.
  - I **never** said you stole the money.
  - I never **said** you stole the money.
  - I never said **you** stole the money.
  - I never said you **stole** the money.

- I never said you stole **the** money.
- I never said you stole the **money**.

That one sentence consisting of seven words could be interpreted with eight different meanings. Now, more than ever, you have to write with crystal-clear clarity in all your communication and leave as little as possible open to interpretation.

- If your team doesn't trust you, none of what you say or do matters anyway.

Varying and often contradictory individual interpretations about what is really important are the primary cause of teams being out of sync. You and your team have to know, without hesitation, "What is really important?" When your team has too many "important" things to focus on, they become paralyzed and take no action at all.

It is up to you to identify what the overriding objectives are that will ultimately determine your team's success and keep the team focused on those main targets. If the attention and energy of your people is being distracted by anything other than the few main things that will lead them to success, that attention and energy is being wasted. In fact, if you are trying to get your team to focus on more than three or four primary targets or objectives, you haven't defined what should be considered primary targets. Wherever you put your focus is where you will get results. Part of your value is in eliminating the clutter— the minor things that get in the way of the really important things.

If the really important things are not crystal clear, each person on your team will do what is comfortable for them to do and the easy/comfortable will trump the important. People will focus on what they perceive as the most important tasks.

When your team's perceptions are not in sync with your expectations you can't expect great results. Chaos will reign.

Simplify

If someone woke you up in the middle of the night and asked what was really important for your success, could you immediately give the correct answer without even thinking about it? How would your team members respond to the same question?

Simplicity liberates your team. Simple does not have to mean short, but it helps. Great wisdom can be stated in four words or less: This too shall pass. Nothing ventured, nothing gained. In God we trust. Let sleeping dogs lie. These are examples of how a complex message can be delivered through a few simple, memorable words.

Many complex, successful organizations simply state why they are in business and what is important to them in just a few words:

Whole Foods: "Whole Foods, Whole People, Whole Planet."

TED: "Spreading Ideas."

Google: "To organize the world's information and make it universally accessible and useful."

Coca-Cola: "To refresh the world."

Nike: "To bring inspiration and innovation to every athlete in the world."

Walmart: "Save money. Live better."

FedEx: "The Purple Promise: I will make every FedEx experience outstanding."

Here are two ways to determine whether your mission is simple and crystal clear—so clear that every member of your team knows exactly what you are trying to accomplish:

1. Does it take you more than 30 seconds to state what is really important?
2. Can you explain what is really important by writing it on a sticky note?

If you answered *no* or *not sure* to either or both of these, your mission is not clear or simple. Your team has to know—without question—what is really important, and you have to constantly, consistently, and clearly communicate that message. It is up to you to develop a simple message that they understand so everyone can achieve the results they want. It is your responsibility to clearly identify what is required—in priority order—to eliminate the stress and confusion created by seemingly contradictory objectives.

Synchronization Begins with You

It doesn't do much good to communicate what is really important unless you are all-in, totally committed, and walk the talk yourself. Simply stated, your "video" must be synchronized with your "audio." Your actions have to be in sync with what you say, or it would be like watching a movie when the audio is three seconds behind the video. Three seconds doesn't sound like much but it frustrates the viewer and destroys the intent of the movie, and the viewer will eventually give up and turn it off.

The best way to create clarity, focus, and synchronization is to include your team in the process of identifying and defining what is really important. If you simply tell your team to "get it done" and do not involve them in the process, you may never hear "this is stupid" until it is too late.

Even though things constantly change, what is really important should not change constantly. Likewise, the actions you reward should be in sync with what is really important. The old management axiom of "What gets rewarded gets done" is still true. That seems so obvious, and yet rewarding the wrong thing is a mistake that many leaders unwittingly make.

To help simplify what is really important, answer three basic questions:

1. Why are we on the payroll—what specific, measurable results have we been hired to achieve?
2. What value do we add to our organization?
3. What are the most important activities we must complete in order to provide that value?

Simplify your really important objectives. Write them down, talk about them, understand what they mean, and let them guide your decisions. When your team answers those three questions, it will simplify your message, clear out the clutter, and eliminate confusion about which things are really important. Simplicity and clarity eliminate chaos and create synchronization.

Unintended Contradictions

Contradictions are an enemy of synchronization. It would be really stupid to purposefully create contradictions; however, unintended contradictions occur all the time. For example, claiming that people are your greatest asset and then eliminating employee training because you "just don't have the time or money" sends a contradictory message. Continually talking about teamwork while implementing programs that pit your team members against each other does the same. And, sometimes you may unintentionally "punish" an idea with cynicism or ridicule, unintentionally sending the message that you are not open to new ideas.

Of course, contradictions are not intentional. Why would anyone want to contradict themselves? Yet unintended contradictions happen within every team. Every action you take creates a reaction . . . make sure that you are not rewarding what you do not want to happen or punishing what you really want to happen.

When your team is in sync with what is really important, they can move with unity of effort toward a common goal.

Don't be stupid. Synchronize.

Don't Be Stupid
Concentrate

"I'm confident that my people know what they're supposed to be doing, but we seem to get less and less accomplished."

—The Leader

"What the heck? Here we go again. We haven't even implemented the last grand plan. I am going to wait this one out; it will soon change back."

—Your Team

The sun emits a billion kilowatts of energy per hour, yet we can deflect most of its harmful effects with an ultrathin application of sunscreen or a visor, which diffuses its energy. On the other hand, a laser beam focuses only a few kilowatts of energy. Yet this relatively weak source of energy can cut a diamond in half or even eradicate certain types of cancer. Your role as the leader is to maintain laser-like focus and concentrate on the things that are important to your success.

If you are like most leaders, your days are filled with clutter. Decluttering is not a new challenge. The source of your clutter may be new, but maintaining concentration and eliminating clutter has been around since the beginning of time. You can spend every hour of every day sorting through the clutter of "things" that pop up every day. Do most of the things that clutter your time and attention help you become the leader you want to become? Maybe not.

The reality is that you have so many things coming at you from so many different directions, you may feel like it is hard to concentrate and get anything done well. As soon as you put out one fire, another one flares up. You may not have any control over the fires, either. Some of the fires may be lit by your boss. Others may be created by your team or members of another department. Regardless of where the fires originate, you feel like you are inhaling smoke all day and not finishing anything that needs to be done. You may feel overwhelmed and, in reality, almost everyone has that feeling. Don't use feeling overwhelmed as an excuse for your lack of concentration on important things.

Just remember, not everything is a crisis and not everything needs immediate attention. So take a deep breath and relax. Your job is not crisis management, and your people should not be firefighters. Don't spread the fires to your team.

Many people fall into a victim mentality whenever something disrupts concentration . . . something that seems to be out of their control. They may even think that there's a grand conspiracy preventing them from doing what needs to be done. In reality, they are their own worst enemy. No matter the situation, you control the next move. Will you sit and simmer about all the fires you have to deal with or concentrate on what is important?

Successful people develop an uncanny ability to deal with the unexpected *and* maintain focus. They recognize that there is no grand conspiracy preventing them from accomplishing what they need to do, and they do not allocate unnecessary resources or attention to fires that are more a distraction than a real emergency. Unexpected fires are going to continue to blaze and you have to figure out how to deal with them. It is your choice whether you decide to be a victim . . . or pro-actively deal with the situation and continue moving forward.

Taking Control

One of the major sources of stress, anxiety, and unhappiness comes from feeling like your life is out of control. No one enjoys that feeling. To take control of your life, you must first take control of your time. Of course, there are some things you can't change about the way you spend your time. You have to wait in lines, at red lights, and for elevators, and there's not much we can do about those things. However, there is a lot you can do about where you concentrate your energy.

There are no magic bullets when it comes to managing your concentration. No one has two or three hours a day they could save by doing one thing better. But everyone can find an hour or two a day they could use better by doing a few things differently. If you want to make better use of your time, look for the small increments of time . . . a minute here, five minutes there, and so on. Add them all up and you'll create more time to concentrate on important things.

Establish Order

A job seldom overworks someone, but people often overwork themselves by making dumb decisions about where they concentrate. Most people can't solve difficulties they have concentrating by working harder. Doing the wrong thing more or harder doesn't help. What you need to do is to find ways to shorten tasks, eliminate steps, combine some tasks, and work easier.

Concentration issues are the result of disorder—chasing temporary priorities. Prioritizing is a full-time job and can be overwhelming at times. Separating the important from the trivial is difficult. It is like playing a never-ending game of whack-a-mole. As soon as you knock one "crisis" down, another pops up.

One common denominator of successful people is that they are extremely organized. They are decluttering experts. They concentrate better because they are really good at four things: identifying priorities, knowing when to say no, attacking procrastination, and making every meeting productive.

Identify Your Priorities

The first step to improving your concentration is to precisely understand your priorities. There's a big difference between concentrating to accomplish priorities and checking off items on your to-do list. Your natural tendency is to do what is fun, convenient, or absolutely necessary at any given time. But your true priorities may not fit into any of those categories. In the absence of clearly defined goals, you'll find yourself involved in trivial pursuits . . . pursuits that will keep you from doing what needs to be done to accomplish your goals while you somehow convince yourself that you're accomplishing something. It's a bad idea to try to fool yourself about how productively you're concentrating.

Ask yourself: If I could accomplish only one thing right now, what would that one thing be? Your answer will help you identify what you should be concentrating on. Write that priority at the top of your to-do list and move everything else down—or completely off—the list.

What about when you have multiple priorities at once? Can you multitask to get them done at the same time? Of course you can multitask if what you are doing is mindless and does not take concentration. However, for important things that require concentration, you can multitask only if you want to do multiple things poorly. Even back in the early part of the twentieth century, Henry Ford believed that a weakness of most people was trying to do too many things at once. "That scatters effort and destroys direction," Ford is noted as saying. "Every now and then I wake up in the morning with a dozen things I want to do. I know I can't do them all at once." When asked what he did about that, Ford replied, "I go out and trot around the house. While I'm running off the excess energy that wants to do too much, my mind clears and I see what can be done and should be done first."

Step one is to identify your priorities and focus your concentration toward those priorities.

Be smart. Important tasks that are your top priorities, most of the time, are not the things that appear to be urgent. Don't be fooled into thinking that whatever seems urgent is worth stealing your concentration from your most important goals. There is not a direct correlation between urgency and importance. Concentrate on the important things and let someone else play whack-a-mole with the urgent crisis.

Know When to Say No

To maintain concentration, you have to know when to say no. Your time and energy are precious resources. Once you spend them, you don't get them back. Saying yes to one thing always means saying no to something else, so it may not be easy to say no, but you are doing it anyway. Successful people create laser-like concentration by saying no to low-priority activities so they can say yes to the things they are really committed to—their top goals and priorities.

Saying no does not mean just saying no to other people. The most important person you can say no to is yourself. Successful people say no and sacrifice the comforts of today—by saying no to something that might be easy, fun, or tempting—so they can concentrate on what is important. They are really saying yes to their ultimate goal.

Saying no is not a once-in-a-while thing, either. Instead, it's a daily, winning habit. For example, if you spend two hours in a meeting that doesn't help your team achieve its goals, that's stupid. If you find yourself frequently saying, "That was a waste of time," or "Boy, that didn't add any value," or "Why was I attending that meeting?," these reflections may be signs you need to start saying no.

The best concentration question you can ask yourself is: "Is this the best use of my concentration at this moment?" If it is, then get busy. If not, then refocus.

Most people keep a to-do list. But just as important as a to-do list is a stop-doing list. Stop doing activities, tasks, reports, meetings, and projects that do not directly support your goals. This will help you concentrate more effectively on the things that are most important.

So why do you find yourself saying yes when you should be saying no? If you're honest in telling someone what your priorities are and why you have to say no, most of the time they will respect that. They would rather hear, "Sorry, I can't do it" up front than "I'm sorry, I didn't get to it" later. Just tell the truth. If saying no could damage your relationship, your relationship with that person is pretty toxic already. Relationships are damaged more by misunderstandings and unspoken perceptions than by disagreements. If you are open and honest, chances are you'll be able to work through an issue of disagreement.

But what about your boss or the people you work with? Sometimes you can't say no to them, but you are still ultimately responsible for achieving results. If it's clear that the activity your boss or team members is suggesting will keep you from accomplishing your priorities, you can say no and explain why you are saying no. If you explain your priorities and they're not in line with the priorities of your boss or team members, something is out of sync.

There is power in understanding your goals and priorities and maintaining a laser-like concentration. Effectively managing your attention boils down to self-discipline. There is no set formula. What works for someone else may not work for you, because your priorities are different. However, if you know your priorities, concentrate, and consistently make the best use of your attention, you'll get more of the right things done.

Attack Procrastination

If you are like most people, when something goes undone it sort of hangs over your head like a dark cloud and is always on your mind. The distraction becomes a concentration buster.

Don't become stressed over what you have to do at the expense of getting things done.

In almost every situation, procrastination is an enemy—a nasty habit that can cost you a lot of time, energy, and frustration. Putting things off seldom improves the quality of your work. In fact, knowing you have something to do that should already be done just increases stress. So to attack procrastination, you have to recognize and admit that procrastination is stealing your time, adding stress to your life, and keeping you from concentrating on your priorities.

If you develop a mindset that there is no better time to get things done than right now, you will get more done in less time. So, do it now! If there's a task you especially dislike and it's a priority, do it first . . . and then, as if by magic, it goes away! If you can't get the entire project done at once, break it into pieces. Your objective is to make progress toward your goal. Taking the first step is the toughest—get moving and your next steps are easier.

Attacking procrastination also means being decisive. When someone says to you, "Call me later and we'll set an appointment," respond by saying, "Let's save ourselves a call and make the appointment now." Then it's done, and you won't have to spend another 10 minutes on a phone call or text exchange just to arrange a meeting. It also seems a lot more sincere, doesn't it?

Managing Your Concentration

Time is a great equalizer; it runs at the same speed for everybody, rich or poor, jet pilot or snail farmer. Time seems to run faster when you're out with friends, slower when you're sitting in the doctor's waiting room. But it's actually chugging along constantly at its normal pace, exactly 168 hours a week, leaving behind a trail of unrecoverable seconds and minutes and hours.

You can't add hours to your day. What you do manage, however, is your concentration—a resource we all possess. As long as you are awake, you produce a continuous stream of concentration.

So, how can you clear out clutter, maintain focus, and become the leader that you want to be? Here are 10 tips that will help:

1. Own your day. Granted, some minutes and hours may already be absorbed by meetings, phone calls, commuting, and so on. However, you still have control over most of the hours in the day. Take ownership of the time you control. Don't make excuses about time. Own your day.

2. Do you know where your time goes? Clutter is the result of not taking the time to clean up the mess. Keep track of how you spend your time for a week. You may be thinking that you do not have the time to track everything you are doing—that is the point. Think of keeping track of your time like a calorie counter—annoying but enlightening. The results will show you where your concentration is invested and where your time is cluttered with unnecessary tasks. Without tracking where your time is going, you will not know what to change. Once you understand the reality of where you are spending your time, you can make better decisions and begin to unclutter your life.

3. Beware of social media. If you are like most users of it, it is an absorber of your concentration, and you may not even know it. Social media covers the gamut—a great way to keep in touch and a great way to waste a whole lot of time. You have to decide if it is worthwhile to you. Just be aware—the use of energy and emotions generated by

social media may be preventing you from becoming the person you want to be.

4. Master specificity. Make it a top priority to eliminate rework. Be specific about what you are asking from someone and what someone is asking from you. Most rework is the result of not answering the basics: who, what, when, and where. That is stupid. Take control of even the small things to avoid rework and frustration.

5. Throw things away. Ask yourself, "What is the worst thing that could happen if I throw this away?" Most of the time, you can live with your answer, so start filling your wastebasket or punching your delete button. Along the same lines, teach your team when to use "reply all." There is a time to use that feature but it is not with every communique. Make a rule, tell your team to hit "reply" unless you specify for them to "reply all."

6. Perfection paralysis is expensive. Sometimes it is not worth the effort to make things "perfect." Take a look at the time costs involved and weigh these against the benefit of perfection. Avoid spending more time than is necessary on things that simply don't require it. If you are like most, you will not get much of anything done unless you move on before things are completely perfect.

7. Time-chunk similar activities together so that you are not starting and stopping all the time. Listen to all your voicemails at once. Return all emails and phone calls at one time. Write all correspondence in one sitting. Eliminate time-consuming transitions from one activity to another.

8. Be candid and learn to say no to things that you do not need to commit to. Thinking that you can wave a magic wand and please everyone is fooling yourself. Being honest upfront and not saying yes to everything will save you time and frustration over the long haul.

9. Go to lunch early or late. Why everyone decides to go to lunch at noon is a mystery to me: they wait on the

elevator, wait in line at the deli, wait in line to get back on the elevator, and then complain about not having enough time for lunch.

10. Reflect and review. Follow Ben Franklin's advice. Begin your day asking yourself, "What good shall I do this day?" End your day answering, "What good have I done today?"

Meetings with Meaning

Every leader has to facilitate meetings. There's nothing intrinsically wrong with holding a meeting. Meetings are necessary to talk about situations, formulate plans, decide on actions, assign roles, and get motivated before something can be accomplished collectively. Then why does the very word "meeting" have such a bad connotation? Because it means "a waste of time" in the minds of many who have suffered through innumerable hours of trivia, irrelevancies, false objectives, personal grandstanding, and boredom.

Meetings are expensive, probably the largest expense without a line item on the income statement. A lot of time, money, and concentration are wasted in meetings. However, a meeting that gets to the point, maintains focus, accomplishes its objectives quickly, and adjourns—in other words, doesn't waste time—is a good investment.

Your team can give you some great suggestions on how they think your meetings could be improved. Listen to them and they will take ownership of making your meetings better. Here are some suggestions to help make your meetings have meaning:

1. Don't fall into the 'perpetually scheduled meeting' syndrome where you're having meetings just because meetings

are regularly scheduled. Make sure every meeting is absolutely necessary. Routine meetings are typically not a good investment.

2. Most meetings can be accomplished in half the time they are currently taking. Author Robert Orben said it best, "Sometimes I get the feeling that the two biggest problems in America today are making ends meet and making meetings end."[1] Touché.

3. Start with the most important and work your way toward the least important items on the agenda. That way you ensure that you cover what you need to accomplish, and you're not rushing through the important items. If you're spending thousands of dollars on a meeting, it is not a good investment to solve a hundred-dollar problem. Focus on what is important and keep moving through your agenda.

Probably the simplest tip that pays the biggest dividend in meeting management is to start and end your meetings on time. It's disrespectful and a bad investment to start a meeting later than scheduled. You waste 30 minutes of productivity by beginning a meeting with 10 people three minutes late. Also, avoid the temptation of recapping when someone shows up late. When you recap, you're rewarding the tardy person and punishing the people who were on time. There should be a penalty for showing up late. Reward the people who made it on time with a well planned, productive session.

End on time. If your meeting is scheduled to end at three, the minute you hit 3:01, everyone begins looking at their watches, wondering how much longer the meeting will last. You can rest assured that your productivity has gone out the window when the scheduled meeting time has passed.

4. Don't fall for the fatigue strategy, where people continue to "sell" their points after a decision has been made. Some people will fight and fight until they wear you down and

you give them what they want. Don't fall for that. Set limits on the time allowed per item and move forward.

5. Eating and meeting? My general rule is to never eat and meet. You either eat or you meet but you can't do both well. If the presentation is worth spending time on, it is worth everyone's attention and not the salad or whatever you are eating. It would be better to have a 30-minute lunch break for everyone to take a breather anyway.

It is a good idea to distribute information for all attendees to read and understand before the meeting or conference call. But, to send out the information with the expectation that the participants read it before the call, and then read it again when the conference call or meeting begins is not a great idea. Why would they read it before the meeting if you are going to read it to them to begin the meeting? That is stupid. Don't re-read the information. Assume that all read what you asked them to read and utilize your time to make forward progress.

Balancing It All

An Italian economist in the 1800s named Vilfredo Pareto observed that 20 percent of the people in Italy controlled 80 percent of the wealth. Then he began looking around and discovered that the 80/20 rule applied to many things. Today it is widely accepted that the Pareto Principle applies in many areas of business, like 80 percent of your results will come from 20 percent of your activities, 80 percent of your complaints will come from 20 percent of your customers, and so on. It definitely applies to concentration, as well.

Your concentration is your responsibility. No one else can accept that responsibility for you. If you aren't able to do the important things, then you're the only one who can make adjustments to solve that problem. Your team is depending on you to be there for them, and that includes making the best use of your concentration.

Conflicting priorities will create chaos in your quest to live a balanced life. You have to work and learn to keep your main thing the main thing—the one overriding priority toward which all of your energy and concentration should be directed at that moment.

I have seen many executives burn out because they try to accomplish an impossible task—getting everything done. You need to take time for yourself and your family. Get to bed early, work hard, but take at least one complete day off work every week . . . and, commit to taking that vacation you've been putting off. Everyone needs rebooting once in a while.

The paradox of concentration is that the more time you take off, the more refreshed you will be to get the important things accomplished. Your energy level will be greater, your attitude will be better, and the people around you will be more productive.

Don't be stupid. Concentrate.

Don't Be Stupid
Value Integrity

"I heard what they said. I'll believe it when I see it."

"You can say that again."
> —Conversation between two employees after
> a communication meeting

The greatest single impact on long-term, positive leadership is integrity . . . the glue that holds all relationships together. Integrity is even more important than being a great communicator. People will go out of their way to avoid communicating with those they do not trust—you are wasting each others' time if there is no trust. Integrity is more important than being charismatic. People will eventually see through charming charisma. The truth will eventually be exposed.

People will begin evaluating your trustworthiness as soon as they meet you. The first question everyone has is "Can I trust this person?" Without trust, no one will take a risk for you. Competence is important, but it matters most after trust has been established.

Many times along your leadership journey you will face an integrity test. It may involve your career, family, or a personal decision . . . but temptation to sacrifice your integrity will come. It will probably appear like a pop quiz, when you least expect it. That is not a pleasant thought, even if you think you are prepared for it.

Adhering to a foundation of integrity is the most important job of a great leader. You can't lead anyone else farther than they are willing to follow you. If you lose your integrity, you have a chance of losing everything.

Integrity Breach—Everyone Is Vulnerable

General David Petraeus was brilliant. After graduating at the top of his class at West Point, his career skyrocketed. He spent 37 years in the army and was a four-star general. One of his last acts in the army was drafting the plan for the surge that stabilized post-Saddam Iraq. Shortly after, General Petraeus was approved as director of the CIA, confirmed with a vote of 94 to 0 in the Senate. He was even considered as a potential presidential candidate.

On November 9, 2012, everything changed. He wrote the following letter to his subordinates:

Yesterday afternoon, I went to the White House and asked the President to be allowed, for personal reasons, to resign from my position as D/CIA. After being married for over 37 years, I showed extremely poor judgment by engaging in an extramarital affair. Such behavior is unacceptable, both as a husband and as the leader of an organization such as ours. This afternoon, the President graciously accepted my resignation.

As I depart Langley, I want you to know that it has been the greatest of privileges to have served with you, the officers of our Nation's Silent Service, a work force that is truly exceptional in every regard. Indeed, you did extraordinary work on a host of critical missions during my time as director, and I am deeply grateful to you for that.

Teddy Roosevelt once observed that life's greatest gift is the opportunity to work hard at work worth doing. I will always treasure my opportunity to have done that with you and I will always regret the circumstances that brought that work with you to an end.[1]

A stellar career ended that day. One of our country's greatest leaders—in his own words—"showed extremely poor judgment" and exhibited "unacceptable behavior." He lost trust. *Brilliant* was not the adjective used to describe David Petraeus after November 9, 2012.

How could that happen? How could a great strategist, brilliant mind, and powerful leader be so stupid? How could he sacrifice his career and family?

While most of us do not have as far to fall in public perception as General Petraeus, lapses in integrity and ethics occur at work every day. Actions that may seem insignificant— stretching the truth to close a deal, gossiping about a team member, adjusting your values based on the situation at hand, submitting questionable expense account reimbursements— all attack your integrity. The reality is that no one is immune to an integrity breach.

Integrity is a byproduct of trust, which in turn is a byproduct of truth and honesty. A breach of trust can cost you everything. To willingly follow someone, people have to be assured that the person they are following is worthy of their trust. When people lose faith and trust in their leaders, everything else goes with it: productivity, job satisfaction, morale, and pride. Loss of trust will completely sap the energy from your team, and it's really tough to restore.

Trustworthy

People recognize integrity when they see it but it is tough to describe. Typically, the words integrity and honesty are used interchangeably. However, *integrity* is a much broader term coming from the word *integral*, which means whole or undivided. If you have integrity you are a complete person. Without integrity you are an incomplete person.

When you install a new software program on your computer, it will automatically run what is called an "integrity check"—a series of tests to determine if any part of the program has been lost or damaged. If any piece of the code in that program doesn't have complete integrity, the program as a whole can't be trusted. At best, you would have a program that doesn't function properly. At worst, using a program lacking integrity could cause you to lose valuable data or even damage your computer, so the integrity check is vital.

Being trustworthy begins with your integrity. Trust, integrity, and honesty are inextricably linked. Are you open and honest? Do you do what you say you will do? When you commit to something, can your team "consider it done"?

There may be a time when you cannot keep your word and do what you said you would do. A situation may have changed, your stance may have changed, or you may have made a mistake and committed to something you should not have. For whatever reason, you cannot do what you said you would do. It happens to everyone occasionally. When that happens, communicate why you cannot live up to your word thoroughly, honestly, and quickly to minimize the damage. Don't make it worse by keeping a promise just to save yourself from looking bad. Acknowledge that things changed, or that you should not have made the promise, or that you did not have the authority to keep your promise.

If people perceive you to be a person of integrity, you will earn their trust over time. On the other hand, if you sacrifice your integrity, nothing else really matters. After all, does it matter what you say to people if they don't trust you? Does it matter how committed, optimistic, skilled at resolving conflicts, or courageous you are if people do not trust you? None of those things matter if you lose your team's trust.

Guarding Trust

Most people do not consider their various interactions with people as unique and isolated incidents. They make judgments and decisions regarding others as if they were personally involved and, if that person is a leader, make the assumption that the leader will treat them the same way. If they perceive that you were fair and reasonable in one situation, they will assume you will be fair and reasonable with them. But the opposite is also true.

Leading with Integrity

The people in your organization judge your integrity every day by what they see you do. When you criticize someone in public, you lose trust. When you encourage people to stretch the truth, your integrity comes into question. When you show favoritism, choose not to return phone calls, say you're out of the office when you're not, or say that you didn't receive a message when you did—you lose trust. Of course, you probably wouldn't intentionally do most of these things, but our intentions really don't matter. What matters is what we do.

If you believe that people will judge you based on your intentions, that is pretty stupid. How do they know what your intentions are? It simply makes no difference how great your intentions are. If there is little or no trust, there is little or no foundation for a successful relationship.

You have to earn your team's trust and constantly re-earn it. The harsh reality is that it may take years to develop trust, yet it can be lost in minutes because of one mistake. You must guard your integrity as your most precious possession . . . because it is.

People judge your integrity on what they see . . . and they either see it or they don't. There are no varying degrees of integrity. You either have it or you don't. There is no such a thing as a minor lapse of integrity. The day-in, day-out, seemingly insignificant things that you do represent the greatest opportunity for integrity erosions. People don't forget integrity mistakes. They will forgive and forget almost any judgment error, but integrity mistakes hang on forever.

Is there ever a time when a small, white lie is small enough that it doesn't really matter? Is there a point at which small lies are okay but big ones aren't? If so, where is that point . . . and how does your team know when they cross the line? The answer is that no lie is so small that it doesn't matter. Lies by commission or omission destroy trust. As minor as a small lie may seem at the time, it has a lasting effect. You cannot pick and choose when you will be a person of integrity. You can't justify a white lie by thinking, "No one was hurt, so it's okay." Once you start making excuses, they will come a little easier each time, and soon you will find yourself on a slippery slope that can lead to an integrity meltdown.

Cornerstones of Integrity

There are four cornerstones that must be upheld if you want to create a culture of integrity. Failure to adhere to any of the four will destroy confidence and trust and your leadership results will crumble.

1. Pursue Truth

A key element of establishing and maintaining your integrity is to discover and then face the real truth—not what you hope to be the truth, but the absolute reality of your situation. Ronald Reagan once said, "Don't be afraid to see what you see." Our nature is to be selective with what we see and to cling to beliefs that are pleasant to us.

Jack Welch, former CEO of General Electric, calls the love of truth the "candor effect."[2] He says that absolute candor from the leader will "unclutter" conversations because people will speak what is actually the truth and not the political rhetoric that goes on in many meeting rooms, boardrooms, and conference calls. The love of truth is an unnatural act worth doing.

Choosing to search for the truth and having the courage to confront the hard realities makes your path a little straighter and the challenges less overwhelming, and you will have fewer surprises along the way. When you punish people for telling the truth you will gradually find yourself surrounded by "yes people" who conceal the truth for their convenience and yours. When the stakes for saying and hearing the truth are too high, your decisions will be based on bad information.

One truth that you have to face is that you cannot do everything. It may sound basic, but overcommitting or committing to something beyond your control will cost you your integrity. Simply doing what you say you will do is one of the principal ways your integrity is judged.

2. Stand Up for What You Believe

To stand up for your beliefs, you have to know what you stand for. What are your core values? What's so important that it will never be compromised for any reason? Your integrity begins when you speak out about what you believe.

People are not good mind readers. If they are left guessing about how you feel or where you stand, they will inevitably be wrong some portion of the time. Openly discussing with your team the uncompromising principles that will exist with every interaction and transaction eliminates the temptation to stretch the truth when they are in the middle of a stressful situation.

Not every decision is black or white. When you are in a gray area, err on the side of fairness. What you do is being closely watched by your team, and their judgments are based on their perception of what they observe. It may not be fair, but you have to manage your people's perceptions. Err on the side of fairness.

3. Live What You Teach

Talking about integrity is easy. Enron, the most tragic business collapse in modern time, listed integrity as one of their core values—along with communication, respect, and excellence. It seems sort of silly now, but Enron spent thousands of hours identifying which values to include on that list. In the end, the list did not mean anything—the way the company was run meant everything.

People react to what they see you do. You can't fake what you teach. The ultimate test of your integrity is whether you do what you said you'd do. Your word and your commitment are judged every time you promise something—regardless of how insignificant you consider it to be.

4. Continually Check Yourself: "What is the right thing to do?"

When I was a young adult, my father was my mentor and role model. When I had a business or personal issue, I would go to him for advice. After explaining the situation, he would ask me a simple question: "Son, what do you think is the right thing to do?" I hated that question. But, I have learned from experience that almost all of the time, I know deep down what is the right thing to do even before asking the question.

How do you know what the right thing to do is? Test yourself by answering these questions:

1. Is it legal, moral, and ethical?
2. Are my actions in sync with my personal and organizational values?

3. How would I feel if this decision were shared in the news?
4. Would it be perfectly okay if someone else made the same decision and it affected me?
5. Am I hiding something? If so, why?

Answering those questions will help ensure in any situation that what you are doing is the right thing to do. Choosing to do the right thing, even when it's painful, will protect your most precious possession: your integrity.

Everything Counts

No matter where you go, people are watching and evaluating your actions. That comes with your leadership title. You may be in the stands at a soccer game, in a restaurant, or on the golf course. Everyone is rating you, just like the Uber driver rates you after a trip.

Be careful with the words you choose. Great leaders do not lead with vulgar, abusive language or use their words as a weapon to insult, criticize, gossip, or speak badly about others in public. Losing control of your tongue will ultimately lead to an erosion of your integrity.

The two basic questions to ask yourself before speaking are: Is it true? and Is it necessary that I share this information? If the situation is true and necessary to share, speak with confidence. If not, it may be best not to say everything you have heard.

Business is personal. If people don't trust you, they won't buy into your leadership. Trust begins with integrity, and without it, nothing else really matters.

People of integrity expect to be believed, and when they're not, they allow time to prove them right. In the words of

President Eisenhower, "The supreme quality for leadership is unquestionable integrity. Without it, no real success is possible, no matter whether it is on a section gang, a football field, in an army, or in an office."

Confidentiality

As a leader, you have access to confidential information that you cannot share with those on your team. How can you earn the trust of your team but also withhold information that affects them? What if you know a layoff is approaching and one of them asks if they will be affected? What if your company is negotiating a merger? What if you are asked why a person on the team was de-hired?

Those are all tough situations, however, there is never a good reason to lie. The best answer is an honest answer: "If I did know, I would not be able to discuss it with you." They may walk away with a false assumption, but that is better than a confidentiality breach. If you have earned their trust over time, they will respect your position and you will maintain your integrity.

Don't be stupid. Protect your integrity like your most precious possession—because that is what it is.

DON'T BE A JERK

"The most important single ingredient in the formula for success is knowing how to get along with people."

—Theodore Roosevelt

The retirement party is in full swing. Associates from throughout the organization have gathered to celebrate and extend best wishes to Bob, a great leader who is retiring. The room is packed.

One by one people go to the front of the room, grab the microphone, and begin talking about the impact that Bob made on them. Some of the stories they tell are funny, some are serious, but every one of them is personal. One person talks about how Bob provided compassion and encouragement

65

during a tough time. Another says that she is thankful that Bob demanded her best and would not accept mediocrity. Some-one else states that Bob listened to him and changed his stance on an issue. Another person remembers the time Bob sent a personal congratulation note to her son for his graduation. Someone else talks about a time that Bob made a serious mistake but owned up to it, learned from it, and became a better leader because of the experience.

Other team members begin their speeches with: *I remember . . .* ; *You took the time to . . .* ; *You helped me . . .* ; *I'll never forget . . .* ; *You cared enough to . . .* ; and so on.

No one spoke about successful or failed strategies. No one mentioned a successful or failed marketing program. There were no toasts to celebrate winning an account. The evening was filled with personal stories of how Bob treated each person individually.

Meanwhile, in the same building, another retirement party is going on. The party is a not a retirement celebration. It is a celebration that a leader has retired. In fact, the leader who is retiring was not even invited to the party. He did the same job and worked just as hard as Bob. But he chose to do it differently. He was a jerk.

Which retirement party do you want?

Bob understood that leadership was not about him. His primary interest was not in the accumulation of power—it was in developing his people to become their very best. The other retiree was more interested in the accumulation of power and wealth than helping those around him become their best. Typically, jerks are greedy and interested in only themselves. They act and react without thinking. Jerks enjoy taking the easy road and are quick to blame others.

That is not you. You are a great person with honorable intentions, but sometimes you may come across differently than what you really are. Unfortunately, everyone occasionally and unintentionally comes across like a jerk. Even Bob appeared to be a jerk at times. The difference in the two retirees was how often they appeared to be jerks and how quickly they recovered when their jerk moment appeared. Bob's jerk moments were rare, temporary, and he recovered from them quickly. His team knew that regardless of the temporary jerk moment, he had their best interest in mind. The other retiree's team knew that his jerk moment was just another ordinary day.

You may be thinking that some jerks achieve extraordinary results. After all, you have heard that nice guys finish last. Yes, some jerks—like Steve Jobs—achieved extraordinary results. He was a marketing genius, fabulous communicator, and incredible visionary yet many of those around him considered him to be a jerk.

Be aware that the people in your organization would probably not stick around for long if you choose the bullying, arrogant, insulting, and uncompromising leadership route.

This part of the book is about your interpersonal leadership. Don't take the harshness of the phrase "being a jerk" personally. The purpose of this part is to provide key areas to focus upon to get better results right now. It will also increase your awareness of what you can do to ensure that you will be invited to your own retirement party when that time comes.

In the meantime, this section of the book will help you focus on things that you can do to get better results right now.

Don't Be a Jerk
Listen Up

"Why do we keep shooting ourselves in the foot? If you would only ask us before you make decisions affecting our team, we could then save ourselves a lot of rework, mistakes, conflicts, and money."
—Anonymous feedback to upper management

In the reality television show *Undercover Boss*, CEOs disguised themselves as new hires and went into the front lines of their organizations to find out what was really going on in their company. There were inspiring stories revealed in some episodes—passionate employees, incredible performance going above and beyond the job requirements, stories of compassion and teamwork. Yet, in many of the episodes, the CEO was shocked to discover that some well-meaning corporate programs were actually punishing people for doing their job. Why were many of the CEOs featured in the show astonished to find that their frontline, hard-working people's needs are not being met? Why were corporate decisions being made without anyone representing the people who were in constant contact with their customers?

Of course, the answer is because the truth was not being communicated from the front line to the executives making the decisions, or the leaders in that organization were not listening. Some of the most painful words a leader can hear from someone on his team are, "I could have told you that wouldn't work."

An extensive study by the Center for Creative Leadership revealed that the two principal behaviors that derail executives are an excessive dose of ego and insensitivity toward the people who are supposed to be following them.[1] A leader who has excessive ego and doesn't care about the most important people in the organization? That sounds like a jerk. A great boss will talk to employees, ask about their job, how can it be done better, and what can they do to help.

Jerks do not listen. If you want answers to your most complex issues, the first place you check should be the room where your team is gathered. Almost every answer that you are looking for is in the very room where your people are waiting for you to ask them.

Think about what consultants do. They are hired to come into an organization and solve a problem. Their first order of business is to listen to people, particularly those on the front line. They listen and listen and listen. People are more than willing to give suggestions to solve the problem. Then, they gather the information, print out a fancy report, and submit it to upper management. The recommendations presented by the consultant were already available to those same leaders, had they been listening.

There is a time and place for consultants. Sometimes a fresh view will provide creative answers. But most of the time, the answers they provide are ones that would have been readily available without an external source asking the questions, had the leaders been listening.

Could it be that your team has the answers you need if you would only ask the questions? After all, who knows more about the issues than the people who are doing the job? Why not ask questions of the people whose decisions you affect?

If you listen to your team and access their creativity and knowledge, everybody wins. Your team just needs to be asked and listened to. The answers are in the room.

Be Present

Even when you are attempting to listen, your team may perceive that you are not with them if you are distracted. When someone is talking to you, be with them. The time for multitasking is not while you are in a conversation. That is the time to focus on the person talking—not reading your computer screen, checking texts, watching things happening outside your window, or checking your to-do list.

The most important and yet the most difficult part of listening is to eliminate mental distractions. Do you remember the last time you did not have something on your mind? You will always have something else on your mind before a conversation begins. One technique to help you be present with the person is to focus on one eye of the person you are listening to. Choose your favorite eye, left or right, but stay focused solely on that eye while you are listening. The one-eye technique acts like an attention tunnel. You will be present with the person. It may sound a little goofy, but try it.

If your communication is taking place over the phone, staying present is even tougher. The distractions are more enticing and you think that the other person is not aware that you are not "all in." The best way to be present when you are communicating over the phone is to take detailed notes. If you outline or diagram what the person is saying, you will automatically focus on the words you are writing and you will be able to stay present.

Be Patient

In my opinion, the most common listening error is to share your point of view too soon. You may want to answer a question even before it has been asked. You may want to deliver your counter argument before the other person has delivered their complete argument. You may get bored and cut them off so you can move on to something more interesting to you. All of those listening errors come across as jerk moments.

Effective listening is not easy. You have to train yourself to be patient while listening because you are thinking at least four times faster than the other person is talking. There will be a time for you to provide additional information or clarification, but be quiet and be patient until you hear all of what the person is saying. Take five seconds to truly process what is being said before you leap into the conversation. Five seconds will seem like a long time but it will help you digest what has been said and formulate your thoughts before you speak.

Unnecessary interrupting—being a "back to me" conversationalist—communicates a clear message that what you have to say is more important, you do not have time to hear the person out, or you don't care what they are talking about. Regardless of the reason for interrupting, you probably come across like a jerk. Check yourself. For one day make a concerted effort to not interrupt. Regardless of your instincts or feelings, don't interrupt. If you implement the "no interruption" rule, even for just one day, three things may happen:

1. You will catch yourself itching to interrupt numerous times during that day. You will probably discover that you could improve your listening patience.
2. You will become aware of how many times other people interrupt you and how rude interruptions are to the person speaking.
3. If you lead your entire team on the "no interruption" day, there is a good chance that others will take your lead and stop interrupting. Your entire organization could change for the better. Try it.

The person talking has real thoughts and feelings, just like you do. If you are talking over their words, those thoughts and feelings will be that you are a jerk. If you don't hear them out before you begin expressing your thoughts, they will probably think you don't care about what they have to say.

Be Active

Have you ever been in a conversation and wondered if the other person was on the same planet with you? They seem distracted, look away, you can tell their mind is wandering somewhere else. It is not a good feeling, is it?

When you struggle to concentrate on what someone is saying, keep repeating in your mind the main message they are attempting to get across. When it is your time to speak, confirm their message and ask questions to connect with them. They have told you what is important to them, so ask questions about what they have said. Don't just jump to a conclusion or solve a problem before you have listened to their point of view.

Your body language should be active as well. Lean forward. Arms open. Nod occasionally. Smile. Focus. Your active body language helps you to concentrate and acknowledges that you are paying attention to what is being said.

Be Interested

As a leader, you do not need to have all the answers to the challenges you are facing. No one has all the answers. But in most cases, your team has the answers. They know how to solve almost every problem. They are closer to the customer and are in the best position to make decisions affecting them.

When you allow your team to have input on issues and you listen with the intent to act on their suggestions, you create positive energy. Involvement in the decision-making process can be a motivator for your people. And the more you involve them, the more they will buy into what your team is trying to accomplish.

It is up to you to create an environment in which they can freely share their thoughts and ideas, and then to listen with an open mind. Sam Walton, a great listener, once said, "I know what I know; I want to know what you know." Another highly successful leader, hotel mogul Bill Marriott, believes the seven most important words a leader can say are: "I don't know . . . what do you think?"

The best leaders are the best listeners. They listen for ideas, not just the facts. But there will be nothing for you to hear if your team isn't talking to you. And if they're not talking, there is a reason. Do they feel comfortable telling you the truth? Or do they think they have to tell you what you want to hear?

Leadership for Breakfast

When I go out to eat, I enjoy great food and great service. It is hard to enjoy great food without great service or great service without great food. They go hand in hand, but I think the most important ingredient of a great meal is a great waiter. A great waiter is present, patient, active, and interested.

Have you ever observed the flurry of activity that a waiter has to manage? Every table they serve has different needs. Some tables comprise senior citizens, others are full of teenagers or young families. And, every table of people are at different stages of their meal: some haven't ordered yet, some are in the middle of their meal, some are eating dessert. Regardless of who is at the table, they all have the same need—to know that the waiter cares about them and their situation right now.

The best resources that a waiter possesses are a friendly smile and the ability to listen to, ask, and answer great questions:

How are you doing today?
What can I get you?
Do you have any questions?

How do you want your meal prepared?
How is your meal?
Is there anything else I can get you?
Are you ready for your check?

Think about each of those questions from a leadership perspective. In your environment, the words may be different but the questions that good leaders ask their team are basically the same:

How are you today?
Is there anything you need from me?
Do you have any questions?
What can we do to make your work environment even better?

Great waiters do not assume that they know the needs of each person. They pay attention, take notes, confirm the order, and follow up after the meal. When your meal is complete, you know your waiter cared about your dining experience. Great waiters teach great leadership. Observe great leadership in action the next time you order at your favorite restaurant.

Don't Lead Naked

One of my favorite stories is the classic fable "The Emperor's New Clothes" by Hans Christian Andersen. As with all parables, the story about the vain and powerful emperor has important lessons for us. You're probably familiar with Andersen's tale, but just in case you're not, the gist is that the emperor is persuaded by mischievous tailors that a magnificent and extremely expensive suit they have produced for him can only be seen by clever people. In reality there is no suit at all, so when the king "wears the suit," he is actually naked.

The crowd at the royal parade was tricked into agreeing that the king's suit is magnificent. No one wanted to appear crazy and be the first to question the "suit." The entire village was persuaded to adopt a completely false belief—exploiting people's pride, fear of embarrassment, and reluctance to be a lone voice of reason.

The tale ends with the intervention of a small boy, who, unaware of the widely publicized mythical claims of the tailors, loudly pronounces the king to be naked, exposing the sham. It took a child to point out the obvious. By then it's far too late to fix the embarrassing situation.

The moral of the story is that you shouldn't get so caught up in your own leadership position that you're afraid or unwilling to ask for and receive feedback. If your team is intimidated by the power of your position or feels pressure to conform to the majority, sooner or later you could end up like the emperor and get caught in an embarrassing position.

If you want to lead fully dressed, follow the example of former New York City mayor Ed Koch. He very famously made an intentional effort to walk around the city every day meeting with the people he served, and asked them, "How'm I doin'?"—a simple question that people respected from their leader.

Another great leadership guru, Peter Drucker, looked back at his 65-year consulting career shortly before he died. He concluded that great leaders all had one thing in common, *"They thought and said **we** rather than **I**."*

It is up to you to create an atmosphere in which your team knows that honest feedback and suggestions are welcomed without recourse. People want to follow a leader who knows that he needs his team more than his team needs him, is secure enough to ask and answer questions, and cares enough to become a great listener.

Don't be a jerk—listen.

Don't Be a Jerk
Make a Decision

"Why don't they do something about this? Everyone knows it is a problem. Why do they stick their heads in the sand?"

"Because that is what they do."

—Two frustrated employees

On January 15, 2009, Captain Chesley "Sully" Sullenberger took off on a routine flight from New York City to North Carolina. The flight would be no different than any of the thousands of other flights that Sully had piloted in his 42 years of flying airplanes—until it was. Two minutes into the flight, everything changed. A huge flock of birds flew directly into both of the plane's engines. More than 3,000 feet in the air, the aircraft lost all power and began slowly losing altitude.

In a flash, Sully was thrown into a situation that he never expected but had prepared for his entire career. He was facing the biggest problem that he would ever have to solve. He did not have to waste time trying to figure out what happened—he saw the birds fly into the engines. What happened was answered, but he had to quickly figure out what to do with the unexpected crisis.

His options were limited. He could attempt to return to LaGuardia airport, where he had taken off, or attempt to do something that had never been safely accomplished before— land in the Hudson River. He quickly made a decision to land in the Hudson. From the time he hit the birds until he landed was only 208 seconds. Only 208 seconds to make a decision, commit to it, and implement it. When the plane landed in the Hudson there was no celebration. A new problem was how to safely get 155 people out of the Hudson River in 21-degree weather and safely on land. With the help of hundreds of first responders, every person on the plane survived that day.

Captain Sullenberger was thrown into a situation that day that was completely unexpected. However, he was prepared. He had the experience and knowledge to make decisions quickly. The crisis demanded a lot of work in an extraordinarily short time. Sully's decisiveness saved his life and the lives of 155 other people onboard that plane.

Decisiveness

Leadership involves decisiveness—understanding your goals and priorities so well that you can make decisions quickly. Many teams slow to a crawl because their decision-making process is slow and weak. Sometimes it is because it is unclear who needs to weigh in on decisions or who has the final authority to make them. And, interestingly, slow decision making can also result when everyone wants to contribute to every conversation and every decision. Inertia sets in as decisions are rethought and redebated.

In both instances, speed is needed. Someone needs to make a decision.

One of the most important attributes you can develop is the ability to confidently make decisions and move forward. Thinking before doing is always, of course, the right thing to do. However, thinking without ever doing leads nowhere. Don't get stuck in an endless thinking loop without transitioning to action: "Ready, aim . . . aim . . . aim . . ." will get you shot and frustrate everyone on your team.

IBM's original motto was simple—Think. In later years they realized that the slogan was out of sync and changed it to make action explicit: Think. Then do. Thinking is only the starting point. First you think, which involves absorbing all the information you can get your hands on. Next, you let your intuition have a go at it, which means *not* thinking about it but letting your mind drift or working on other things until the answer becomes clear to you. This could happen the moment you wake up in the morning or simply out of the blue when you're thinking about something else entirely. Then, you act.

You can't eliminate problems or prevent adversity from attacking your team. No one expects you to wave a wand that would make any problem magically disappear, but problems don't just go away. Don't be a jerk and ignore problems. The quicker you address them the better chance you have to prevent them from destroying your team.

Contingency Planning

The best problem-solving technique is to address the potential problem before it becomes real and you're in the middle of a crisis. You can think more clearly and evaluate alternatives better before things go haywire.

There may be a time when you have to solve a life-changing crisis that had never been solved before, like the decision Captain Sullenberger made in January 2009. However, most pilots do not make new decisions while they are in the middle of a crisis. They implement plans that were created before the crisis. For example, if a light flashes, signaling a hydraulic problem on the aircraft, the pilot opens the manual and finds the procedure for correcting the problem. Then he implements that procedure. It is almost impossible for a pilot to think of everything he might need to do while he's stressed in a crisis and the plane is going down.

The same logic applies to your leadership. Sometimes you may see lights flashing, indicating a problem. When that happens, some people will try to ignore it by throwing a rug over the light so they can't see it flashing anymore. Your team sees the problem at least as clearly as you see it, so ignoring or hiding the problem is never a good idea. If you ignore the issue, your team will think you are a jerk.

Other people may unscrew the bulb . . . no more annoying flashing light. They may even pass the bulb to another department. But when they check the other business gauges, the team is still losing altitude.

Some may smash the light with a hammer. That makes them feel better temporarily, but the team is still going down and you just destroyed a person's career.

The only way to fix the problem is to go directly to what's causing the light to flash and solve it. Ideally, an action plan has been decided on before the crisis developed. When you are in the middle of a crisis, your vision is cloudy and it is easy to justify going down the least painful path. But the problem won't just go away. You have to take action.

The Last to Know

Many times you are the last to know about a problem on your team. Even then, what you finally see is normally a small part of the whole. It is like seeing an iceberg in the ocean. Above the water you can see the tip, but what lies below is much larger, more powerful, and usually much more destructive.

If you think dancing around a problem doesn't matter, think again. You're always leading, even when you think no one else is looking. Your team doesn't really care if your organization has an ethics department or compliance officer; what matters to them is that you make a decision to address the problem.

Two common attributes among successful people are: (1) they do not make excuses to justify why things are the way they are, and (2) they don't complain that things aren't as they should be. They accept reality and take charge to make positive things happen. It is easy to get caught in the excuse trap. Don't let that happen. You will always be able to find others to agree with your excuse, but it will never solve any problem.

Dealing with Interpersonal Conflicts

Most problems inside organizations involve interpersonal conflicts within a workgroup. Very few of these conflicts work themselves out without intervention, and your intervention consumes a lot of your time, energy, and enthusiasm.

If you are breathing, you've probably experienced the consequences of conflict in the workplace: a project that was derailed; productivity drained; missed targets, goals, and deadlines. Just one incident can be so stress-inducing and unpleasant that it wipes out an entire week. One leader observed, "When someone comes to me about a conflict, everything stops. I have to turn away from my work and help them. The time and energy it takes to step in and help them work something out is very draining. And the rest of the team is watching—they usually know about the conflict before it ever gets to me."

It's no wonder conflict is a huge pain in the neck.

Problems handled calmly, skillfully, and with speed are opportunities to create positive change. It stimulates creativity and problem solving. In fact, too little conflict, settling for the status quo, may be just as harmful as too much conflict.

Molehills to Mountains

A manager was once promoted to a job on a large rig in the middle of the ocean. He was asked if there was a difference in leading people while on land or on sea. "There is a big difference," he replied. "When you are at sea, if there is a problem and you do not jump on it, someone is going overboard."

Whether you are leading your team on land or at sea, the key to managing conflicts is to address them quickly, or something bad is probably going to happen. As tempting as it may be, don't make the mistake of hoping the conflict will just go away. The longer it is allowed to fester, the more it grows, the harder it is to solve, and the more energy is spent trying to resolve it.

A rule of thumb in dealing with conflicts is called the 1-10-100 rule. The concept is that the longer a conflict exists without being addressed, the more expensive and time consuming it will be to fix. For example, if a conflict between two people is solved quickly and efficiently, it can be solved with the equivalent of *1* unit of time, money, or resources. That same problem—if it's not addressed and spreads throughout a workgroup—will require the equivalent of *10* units of time, money, or resources to solve because more emotions and perceptions must be addressed. If the problem spreads throughout the organization or into the customer base, it will require at least *100* units of time, money, or resources to solve. That is 100 times what it would have cost to solve the same conflict in the beginning. In other words, what began as a molehill has been allowed to grow into a mountain.

When your decision is to make no decision, there is no energy moving forward. Small issues grow and grow. The more an issue grows, the more difficult and time consuming it is to fix and the more of your energy it will consume.

The 1-10-100 rule applies to many situations—a minor conflict between two team members, a billing discrepancy with a customer, a quality slippage, or a simple misunderstanding with a vendor. An old proverb stated: "Never leave a nail sticking up where you find it." In other words, don't just ignore minor problems, hoping they'll go away. Put speed to work to resolve small conflicts quickly, before they become expensive and frustrating disasters.

The only exception to the rule of handling conflicts quickly is when you are personally involved. In those situations, the best strategy is to put some time between the other person's action or behavior and your own. Give yourself some time to clear your head, calm down, and think through the alternatives rationally.

Find Solutions Quickly

Here is a simple process that you and your team can use to find solutions quickly and effectively:

1. Take the time to clearly identify the problem. Most people jump to a solution before they understand precisely what the problem is. As a result, they solve the wrong problem or try to solve a problem that doesn't exist, while allowing the real problem to pick up steam.
2. How do you know if you're solving the right problem? The key is to involve as many people as possible in obtaining the facts necessary for a long-term, effective solution. Seldom does the leader have access to all the facts; ask specific questions to anyone who can provide all the pieces of the puzzle.
3. Write down exactly what the problem is and the impact it has on your team. Be specific. For instance: The problem is that our customer retention rate has decreased by 10 percent—1,000 customers—this year and because we are losing customers, we will have to decrease our expenses, beginning immediately.
4. Write down what you want to accomplish—your desired end state. For example: Our mission is to increase our customer retention by 20 percent over the next 12 months. Once you've gone through those steps, you have everything you need to begin looking for solutions to the problem.

5. Write down why you think the problem exists and some potential solutions. For instance: The problem exists because we rewarded less work, paid more for new business, ignored our existing customers, had 30 percent more turnover in our department, and so on. You'll be surprised how often new options surface when you know exactly what the problem and its impact are, what you'd like to accomplish, and have a clear understanding of what created the issue you are facing.

6. The last step is to identify specifically whose help you need and what you need from them. If you follow each of those steps you will clearly understand the problem and the actions you need to take to solve it.

Dealing with Adversity

Every team will face adversity. If allowed, it will literally consume your thoughts, actions, and enthusiasm. Adversity can strike faster than a death adder snake that can go from a strike position, to injecting venom into its prey, and returning back to the strike position all in 0.15 of a second. It strikes so swiftly that the victim does not immediately realize that they have been bitten. In 0.15 of a second, a life is changed forever. So it is with adversity.

A few months ago I was at a meeting of highly successful leaders and the topic of adversity was discussed. Within that group, people had faced cancer, suicide, divorce, loss of children, drug abuse, loss of spouse, significant health issues, loss of jobs, bankruptcy, and other major areas of disappointments. Each person had faced a major crisis.

Remarkably, every single person agreed that overcoming personal or professional adversity was a critical turning point in their success. Think about that. Adversity turned them toward success. Regardless of how the adversity arrived, those successful people took action, faced, attacked, and conquered the adversity that struck them. Adversity polished them up to become more successful. They made a conscious choice to spend their energy attacking their situation and moving forward.

When confronted with adversity, you can choose to see the positive alternatives and become even better than you were before—or you can choose to sit and dwell on your circumstances for the rest of your life. Spending your energy complaining, justifying, and blaming others for the problem changes nothing and will drain the energy needed to begin working your way through your adversity.

One of the greatest dangers while facing adversity is to panic, freeze, and stop moving forward because you perceive the situation as insurmountable. Regardless of how bleak the situation appears, there are alternatives that will help you move forward if you choose to see them. Make a decision to just keep moving.

Along Germany's famous high-speed Autobahn, many accidents are caused by people who are driving too slowly. Without keeping up the pace, they get run over. The same theory applies in leadership, where reacting too slowly, or not at all, will paralyze your team. It is your job to make a decision, solve problems quickly, and deal with adversity that comes your way. Your team is depending on you.

Don't be a jerk. Make a decision.

Don't Be a Jerk
Answer Why

"Why are we doing this?"

"I have no idea. It makes no sense to me, either."
— Email exchange between two employees

Why? is a simple question. If you are a parent, it is a question that you may have tired of hearing from your three-year-old. Even at that age, the question made sense to the toddler, though your answer may not have been acceptable to him. The fallback line of "because I said so" may have been okay at the time for the toddler, but that it didn't work too well with your teenager, did it? It's not a good line to try on your team, either.

From a young age, people seek meaning for doing the things they do. Everyone has an innate need to know why things are the way they are, work the way they work, and what difference it makes. Understanding why provides purpose and direction. Everyone will move forward together only after "why" is clearly understood.

A leader's reluctance or refusal to answer why is a source of frustration, apathy, and aggravation. It is easy for your team to criticize a decision if they only know what you decide and not why you decided it. If you cannot answer why you are asking someone to do something, then you need to ask yourself why.

Understanding why changes perspectives. Stephen Covey shared a story to emphasize how a person's perspective can be changed in an instant—even when unexplainable things are happening—if they understand why:

> I remember a mini-Paradigm Shift I experienced one Sunday morning on a subway in New York. People were sitting quietly—some reading newspapers, some lost in thought, some resting with their eyes closed. It was a calm, peaceful scene. Then suddenly, a man and his children entered the subway car. The children were so loud and rambunctious that instantly the whole climate changed.
>
> The man sat down next to me and closed his eyes, apparently oblivious to the situation. The children were yelling back and forth, throwing things, even grabbing people's papers. It was very disturbing. And yet, the man sitting next to me did nothing. It was difficult not to feel irritated. I could not believe that he could be so insensitive to let his children run wild like that and do nothing about it, taking no responsibility at all. It was easy to see that everyone else on the subway felt irritated, too.
>
> So finally, with what I felt was unusual patience and restraint, I turned to him and said, "Sir, your children are really disturbing a lot of people. I wonder if you couldn't control them a little more?"

The man lifted his gaze as if he was becoming conscious of the situation for the first time and said softly, "Oh, you're right. I guess I should do something about it. We just came from the hospital where their mother died about an hour ago. I don't know what to think, and I guess they don't know how to handle it either."

Can you imagine what I felt at that moment? Suddenly I saw things differently, I felt differently, I behaved differently. Everything changed in an instant.[1]

Understanding why trades confusion for clarity. It eliminates misinterpretations and miscommunication and provides a clear and precise purpose.

Why Do We Do What We Do?

Excellence and passionate performance is delivered by people who have an understanding of knowing why their work makes a difference. People have a basic need to understand why they need to do what they do and how they fit into a worthwhile cause. Answering why ignites passion, which exposes opportunities.

Maybe you've heard the story about three people working side by side on a construction job. All three people were asked the same question: "What is your job?"

The first person never looked up, but said, "My job is to do what I am told for eight hours so I can get a check."

The second person replied, "My job is to crush rocks, and I am a great rock crusher."

The third person looked up and said with pride, "My job is to build a cathedral."

Three people—all doing the same job, but with completely different perspectives. Which of the three do you think would be the best long-term employee? Although the first person is versatile and dependable and the second can be a grand rock crusher on other projects, the third person will likely be the most committed. The odds are he will have a greater sense of job satisfaction because he understands why he is crushing rocks all day and how his crushed rocks fit into a worthwhile cause.

Answering why creates energy. When people understand why what they do is important, they will focus on the end result—building cathedrals—rather than just crushing rocks.

Sharing Knowledge

When your team understands the vital signs of the business, they're better able to buy into why decisions are made and accept them as logical, even though they may not necessarily agree with every decision. Sharing knowledge is the basis for building understanding—the foundation to acceptance and support. It changes the way people perceive their work. Although your team may not specifically ask, they want to know if they are winning . . . or not.

Leaders who invest the time to teach their team the critical factors of the business get better results. Start with the basics. The numbers are more than digits on paper—they are the gauges that communicate results and determine success. They indicate how well your team is doing, identify areas for improvement, and allow your team to see how their day-to-day activities affect your organization and your customers.

Many leaders want to share the vital signs of the business only on a "need-to-know" basis or to hide them from co-workers altogether. Keeping this "intelligence" solely at your level doesn't make sense. You can't utilize the power on your team until you share your knowledge. It allows them to see things through a wide-angle lens and become more aware of where they fit in and why they are important. The more information you share about the "why" behind the "what" you are trying to accomplish, the better it will be for everyone.

Peter Drucker once said that everyone should know the answer to these two questions:

"What is our business?" and "How is business?"

Those are two great questions. If you can answer those two questions, you can answer why to almost every question your team will have.

The 95/5 Rule

In early America, silos were familiar structures across the landscape. They were tall, cylindrical structures, usually standing beside a barn. Silos had no windows and were used to store grain. The silos were sealed to exclude air and were used for making and storing silage.

In business, teams often operate as silos—separate, distinct, and isolated from the rest of the organization. People work in their own silos, communicate only with people inside their silo, and have little contact with people in the rest of the organization. Teams working in silos can destroy your organization.

Most workgroups inadvertently operate under the "95/5" rule, meaning that individual teams understand about 95 percent of what goes on inside their own department, but only

5 percent of what goes on in other parts of the organization. The teams within specific disciplines—such as sales, human resources, accounting, operations, R&D, and so on—become isolated from other business units. This isolation can result in uninformed decisions that negatively impact everyone.

Of course, it is unreasonable to expect teams to know everything about what goes on within other workgroups. But is it unreasonable for each team to know so little about the rest of the organization and how all the pieces of the picture come together? Wouldn't things work better if everyone could see a bigger picture? Absolutely. They would have a better understanding of why they have to do things the way they do. If you "tear down the walls" between departments and increase understanding from 5 percent to 10 or 20 percent, your team will become more engaged with a mission greater than just their own team.

Tumbleweed or Redwood

You've probably worked with some great (and not so great) leaders. One person I learned a lot from was the least effective leader I've ever seen. His method of leadership was to pit the teams within his organization against each other—sales was bad for operations, operations was bad for sales, finance was the enemy to all. Needless to say, there was no sense of teamwork. He said and did whatever was on his mind at the time without considering the impact. It sounds crazy, but that was the way he led. He was a jerk who led his company straight into bankruptcy.

His leadership philosophy is tumbleweed leadership. If you've ever been to a dry, arid climate like Arizona, you've probably seen tumbleweeds . . . blowing here and there, in all different directions. A tumbleweed is an above-ground plant that, once mature and dry, disengages from the root and tumbles in the wind. It has no control over where it goes—the wind is in charge. There is no logic for why the tumbleweed goes where it goes.

Tumbleweed leadership will destroy your team. Without the roots of understanding what and why, your team members will tumble here and there, with no sense of direction other than where the wind pushes them that particular day.

In contrast to tumbleweeds are redwood trees. Have you ever seen a magnificent redwood tree? Growing over 300 feet tall they tower above all other trees. Most of them have scars on their trunks reflecting tough times; some even have huge caverns carved through their trunks by wildfire. But still they grow. Redwoods are so full of life that it's difficult to kill one.

The secret to the redwood's amazing ability to survive and endure is not in the individual tree itself. Redwoods grow in clusters; their strength is their root system. You might think that redwoods are able to grow so tall because of their deep roots, but in fact, they have no taproot and their roots may reach no deeper than 6 to 12 feet. For every foot in height, the redwood tree sends its roots three times that distance . . . not down, but out. If the tree is 300 feet tall, its roots go out 900 feet, intertwining with the roots from the other redwoods in the grove.

Redwoods can withstand the elements and even the ravages of fire because they are connected. The roots in a grove are so interwoven that it's impossible to tell which roots belong to which tree. Standing alone, an individual redwood could easily fall; but intertwined and standing together, they strengthen and support each other. Each tree is independent, but they are connected through their roots by a common goal—survival.

Leaders who connect and intertwine their team members by answering what and why practice redwood leadership. These leaders consistently reinforce what is important and why it is important, and they place great emphasis on teamwork and constantly let their teams know how they are doing. These are the roots that hold the team together. Team members are aligned, support each other, and are accountable to one another. High-performing teams are redwood teams.

There is a stark contrast between tumbleweed leadership and redwood leadership. The tumbleweed is dried up and dead; it goes wherever the winds take it. The redwood is strong, always growing higher, connected to all the other trees in the grove. When you link your team together with shared knowledge, and answer why they are asked to do what they do, they have a better chance to withstand whatever comes their way.

Don't be a jerk. Answer why.

Don't Be a Jerk
Encourage

"My manager never returns my calls. She only calls me when it fits her agenda. That drives me crazy."

"I don't think she really cares."

          —Conversation overheard at airport terminal

Both of those people may stay with their organization for a long time, but I wouldn't bet on it.

In Maslow's hierarchy of needs, two of the most significant psychological needs we have as human beings are the need to be appreciated and the need to belong. These needs are met through encouragement and recognition.

Oftentimes leaders get so focused on the "big things" that they forget to take care of the basics, like showing the people on their team that their leader actually cares about them. As the poet Robert W. Service said, "It isn't the mountain ahead that wears you out; it's the grain of sand in your shoe."[1] Many times the "grain of sand" that keeps someone disengaged at work is lack of attention and encouragement from their leader.

William James, recognized as the father of American psychology, stated that the most fundamental psychological need is to be appreciated.[2] Everyone has the need to be appreciated. The unspoken question from your team is, "Do you care?" What they mean is, do you care about them as a person—as more than just another cog in the company wheel?

You are already answering the "Do you care?" question, whether you know it or not. Even if you are not consciously and verbally answering the question, it is always being answered by what the people on your team see you do. Of course, it is never your intention to create an environment where your team assumes you don't care about them, but that may be the signal you're sending nonetheless. We sometimes have a blind spot and believe that we are more appreciative of our team than they think we are. Perhaps that is why many leaders are surprised when an unexpected resignation hits their desk.

When people are in the midst of uncertainty, are overworked, feel they are carrying a disproportionate share of the load, or believe they are being mistreated, they immediately assume you do not care. That isn't fair, but that's just the way it is.

The main reason that great people leave good organizations is simply because their need for respect and appreciation is not being met. Their perception is that they work hard and do the right things, yet nobody pays attention. People leave *people* long before they leave organizations. They give up hope that their leader will ever meet their needs. They conclude that a leader they know nothing about will be better than the one they know.

If you are expecting a paycheck to answer their need of appreciation, you will be sorely disappointed. Even a raise in pay is only a short-term boost at best. Money is the most expensive and least efficient way that you can show your appreciation.

Conversely, the least expensive and most effective way is to invest your time and attention with your people. One of your top priorities as a leader is to be available for your team. If you are always busy in "management land," you send the signal that everything else is more important than your team. If you spend your time just drilling down into the numbers, they will assume you only care about the numbers. That is a bad signal to send to the people you need to perform in order for you to be successful.

Do You Care?

"Do you care?" is a personal question asked by *individuals* on your team. That means you must answer the question *individually*. You must give your time and attention to what is important to each of them, not what is important to you or to their teammates.

We are connected today as we've never been before. We are texted, emailed, blogged, instant-messaged, LinkedIn, Facebooked, Twittered, mapped, GPSed, web-enabled, iPhoned, and Googled with real-time information and news. Earth-orbiting satellites know where we are every second, how many inches we are from our favorite restaurant, and whether our airbags have deployed. We are connected to technology, but not necessarily to one another.

Technology is a great productivity enhancement tool for many aspects of leadership, but it can be a detriment to building personal relationships with your team. You cannot build solid business relationships electronically. Answering the basic question, "Do you care?" involves a one-on-one expression in person or, at minimum, on the phone. A handshake and a look in the eyes to say "thank you" has a far greater impact than any message on a screen.

Managing the Climate

In every workgroup, there is a climate—positive or negative that exists. Your role is to continually adjust the temperature to provide your team with the most productive climate in which they can grow. Just as managing the temperature in a greenhouse provides plants the right environment to grow, you control the thermostat for your team.

A climate exists in your organization even before you do anything. The current climate can be positive or negative but it already exists and the temperature changes frequently. Sometimes you may not know exactly what the climate currently is, but it's there, whether or not you are aware of it.

In addition to adjusting for a changing climate every day, as the leader you personally *always* affect the climate. Whether you know it or not, everything you do and even things you don't do affect the climate. Most people are aware of how they affect the climate with their actions, but many leaders underestimate the impact they have on the team when they take no action. You control the thermostat and the environment both by what you do and what you don't do.

So, how can you create a growing, productive, positive environment? The best way is for you to *provide consistent encouragement*. But before you even begin to adjust your thermostat with encouragement, you are wasting your time if each person on your team does not know what to do and why they should do it. Not knowing what and why will counter any great encouragement you could provide. Without answering what and why, your team's climate will settle at whatever temperature level each person is the most comfortable with.

Long-term climate change requires consistent encouragement. It does not have to be major or expensive—everything counts; even "small" things matter.

A simple thank-you note written to an employee at home matters.

A phone call when someone is going through a personal crisis matters.

A compliment in front of peers matters.

A phone call on their birthday matters.

Asking about their family matters.

Your team needs to know they matter to you.

Your encouragement must be *sincere, specific, timely, and personal*. If you're not sincere, people will see through you like a crystal glass. Insincere praise will have a negative effect on the climate. Most people are experts (or at least think they are) at reading the sincerity of their leader. Faking positive encouragement is risky. Be sincere, or wait until you can be.

If you're not specific with your encouragement, you are probably wasting your time. Telling someone "good job on your project report" is okay, but what behavior would you want them to repeat—specifically, what constituted a "good job"? But if you tell them "thanks for your excellent detailed report on the project. I especially liked the way you outlined the action plan required for next week," then you have told them what is specifically important to you. The words "I especially liked" are great words to begin your specific feedback.

Your encouragement must be *timely*. The quicker you provide encouragement after the behavior you're trying to reinforce, the better your results will be. If you wait too long, they will begin to assume that you really didn't care. Then you'll have to work twice as hard to get the climate back to where it should be.

Your encouragement must be *personal*. Don't try to encourage your team members with something that's important to you but not to them. It doesn't do you any good to reward someone with something that they couldn't give a flip about, no matter how important it is to you. In fact, it may do more harm than good. I learned this the hard way a few years ago when I "rewarded" a top performer with tickets to a football game. Those tickets were extremely important to me and I proudly created a contest for my team. The winner would receive my "valuable" tickets to the game.

The person who won the contest was not a football fan. As unbelievable as it was to me, he didn't even know about the game. He went to the game, but it didn't mean much to him. I later found out he was a movie buff. He would have been happier if I'd given him tickets to a movie. It would have cost me a lot less; more importantly, it would have been more meaningful to him, and he would have had a lot more fun. The lesson? Recognition is in the eye of the beholder. If you want to show you care, demonstrate it with things that are important to the individual.

Recognition doesn't have to be formal, and it doesn't have to be a big deal. There are a gazillion ways to improve the climate on your team. One upscale hotel in California, Joie de Vivre Hotel, provides their "employee of the month" with a children's book, *The Little Engine That Could*. You may remember the book: "I think I can. I think I can. I think I can." And finally he does. It may sound silly that something so elementary and simple would matter to adults, but it does. Of course, it is not the book or the story that matters. What matters is the personal note written in the book by Chip Conley the CEO recognizing their positive performance. No matter your budgetary constraints, you can always find ways to encourage your team. Find the encouraging actions that work best, and then use them often.

Controlling the climate on your team is a full-time job. Your team is probably surrounded by discouragers—the world is full of them—and they like to get their hands on everyone else's thermostat. Although they do not influence your team as much as you do, they can mess up the climate with their cynicism, negativity, and pessimism. Keep an eye on who is trying to negatively adjust your team's thermostat and address the situation.

When you create a climate of personal growth and success, everyone will enjoy growing and succeeding. One of the greatest gifts for yourself and others is to encourage people by lifting them up. When you encourage your team every day, don't be surprised if they begin asking you what they can do to help encourage you. That's the way it works. The more encouragement you give, the more others will encourage you.

Don't be a jerk. Encourage.

Don't Be a Jerk
Attack Complacency

"Hey, we are doing pretty good. Why would we want to make any changes?"

"Don't you think we could do a little better?"

—Sometimes star questioning his leader

In the 1970s Kodak and Xerox were the toast of American technology. Both companies were headquartered in Rochester, New York, and if you lived in Rochester during that time, you probably worked for one or the other. It was a boomtown. Kodak dominated the camera, film, and picture development market; Xerox dominated the copier market. Times were good.

Charles Simonyl was a programmer for Xerox at their research facility in Palo Alto, California. The team at Palo Alto

Research (PARC) invented word-processing software graphics that displayed multiple-sized fonts on a screen. The graphics were referred to as WYSIWYG or "What you see is what you get." The intuitive software was manipulated by a computer mouse. Simonyl left Xerox in 1980 to join Microsoft because "Xerox didn't have the right answers to complex technology questions. That's normal," he said, "but what bothered me the most was that they didn't know the right questions, either." In the meantime, 24-year-old Steve Jobs negotiated with Xerox to visit the PARC location. He then cherry-picked the talent at PARC for Apple. Xerox was the inventor of the personal computer, intuitive software, and the mouse. It was not a big deal to Xerox—things were going well. The PARC was way out there—both in location and the traditional thinking at Xerox.[1]

In 1975, Kodak employee Steven Sasson invented the first digital camera. It was more complicated than the cameras of today but created pictures without film. It was revolutionary but was resisted by Kodak's marketing department, who knew that they could sell the digital camera but feared that it would cannibalize their film sales. At that time, every aspect of the photography business was dominated by Kodak. Photography prints had been Kodak's bread and butter for over 100 years; printing was an expensive process and no one was complaining about it. Sasson was prohibited from speaking publicly about his invention or showing anyone outside of Kodak his proto-type. Kodak was 15 years ahead in the digital game but put Sasson's digital invention in a closet. Canon, Olympus, and Nikon left Kodak behind without a fight. In 2012, Kodak filed for bankruptcy protection and later that year announced that it would cease making digital cameras.[2]

Intuitive software, the mouse, and digital cameras could have been dominated by the inventors of the technology. Instead they were ignored. Xerox and Kodak are no longer the toast of technology; they are just toast in technology. Both great companies became complacent and failed to move forward with new, innovative products that they invented!

Complacency is the root of mediocrity.

When Mediocrity Sets In

A dose of success is comfortable. You might not notice this in yourself, but it's easy to see in others—for instance, how many times have you watched athletic teams take a lead and then lose the game because instead of playing to win, they began playing not to lose? They pull back and start playing cautiously, losing the intensity that earned them the lead. Before long the lead evaporates.

Being comfortable for too long can work against you. It's safe in the comfort zone—you know the boundaries and the landscape. There is little or no risk; a misstep here or there is no big deal. But nothing big is won in the comfort zone. The risk is small, but so is the reward.

Mediocrity is success's worst enemy—a greater enemy than failure. Mark Zuckerberg, Facebook CEO and founder, may have said it best: "In a world that's changing really quickly, the only strategy that is guaranteed to fail is not taking risks." If viewed with the right perspective, failure leads to success because it forces you to move in another direction. Mediocrity, on the other hand, hinders success because it keeps you in your comfort zone and prevents your team from moving forward.

Learning and growth happen when you are uncomfortable. Think of your most defining moments in your life. Were you hanging out in your comfort zone? Probably not—I bet you were hanging over the edge.

If you feel your team settling into a comfortable routine, ask yourself, "Are we getting complacent? Are we too comfortable?" When you are complacent, you have to let go to grow. You have to be willing to purposely seek learning opportunities at the edge of your comfort zone. It's not natural to choose to be a little uncomfortable, but the best leaders do it anyway. Growth and success are optional, and if you choose that option, you will have to continue to change.

Change Is Good . . . Your Turn

Many people would rather do anything than change . . . even when things may not be going well.

Do you remember reading a book in high school titled *The Road Less Traveled*? Three words were on the first page of the book: "Life is difficult."[3] The reason the road was less traveled was because it was difficult. People would pass it by looking for the road without difficulties—Easy Street. Responding to change is like going down the road less traveled. It's not Easy Street but it gets you where you need to be.

Most people say, "If it's not broken, don't fix it!" Why waste time fixing something that's not broken when there are usually plenty of other things that really do need fixing? Sometimes it is best to leave something that is working alone.

But eventually there will come a time when adjustments need to be made. Even when it is not completely broken yet, most things can be improved. Some people hunker down and refuse to change, regardless. Their motto is, "I'll keep doing everything exactly as I've been doing it."

Maybe there is a better, more productive way to look at change. John F. Kennedy once said, "You fix the roof when the sun is shining." A better way is not to wait until the storm does its damage before reacting to something that will eventually need to be fixed.

Stress regarding change is perfectly normal and natural. The success of any change depends, in large measure, on your attitude about that change. Every time you lead your team through an exit, you have an opportunity to make a grand entrance into a new opportunity. The only way for you to enter the next level of your success is to exit the current level. That's what change does—it exits the status quo and enters a new beginning.

You cannot make changes without having the courage to exit the comfortable. Courage is having the guts and the heart to do things differently for the sake of progress. Improvement doesn't happen by taking the path of least resistance or conforming to the way things have always been done. It takes courage to lead people through change and maintain focus.

Change is not new and it is not going away. Heraclitus is credited with stating "The only constant is change"—in 500 BC. He probably didn't make it up. He probably got it off the side of a cave wall somewhere.

The changes Heraclitus faced were different than the challenges today. Nevertheless, leading people through change almost 2,000 years ago undoubtedly came with its own unique set of challenges and difficulties. Everyone inherently resists change in varying degrees and, clearly, the message of Heraclitus is: Exit the ways of the past and enter the path toward improvement for the future.

Moving Through the Exit Door

Change is hard on everyone. The exit door is tough to get through sometimes, even though what you are entering may eventually make you more successful. Most people enjoy stability and comfort. Change typically represents the opposite—discomfort and instability; few people enjoy traveling into those regions.

Regardless of how anyone feels about it, change is necessary for improvement.

There are two important lessons to learn about change.

First, if your situation changes—even if your needs have always been met and you are comfortable with the old way—react to the change. All through your life you have seen things change and improve. You exited dumbphones and entered smartphones. You exited maps and entered detailed directions available on your handheld device. You exited albums and entered personalized music. You exited wires and entered wireless. You were doing okay the old way, but everyone would agree that those exits led to grand entrances.

Positive change is not unique to technology. Look around. Look at the workplace, or your family and friends. Things have changed. If you are waiting for things to be like they used to be, you could wind up miserable. Jeff Bezos, founder of Amazon, said, "What we need to do is always lean into the future; when the world changes around you and when it changes against you—what used to be a tailwind is now a headwind—you have to lean into that and figure out what to do because complaining isn't a strategy." When your situation changes, don't sit and wait—be courageous enough to exit and enter.

But, Times Are Good . . .

The second lesson to be learned is that while your needs are being met, keep looking for ways to improve. When things are going well, keep changing. You can only improve if you are making positive changes.

Change is not going away. In fact, there will probably be more changes in the next 10 years than there have been in the past 50 years. Basically everything you use today will be obsolete in five years, so be prepared. Your leadership through change will have a major impact on your success and the success of your team.

Hero or Jerk?

What can you do to be a hero rather than a jerk when you lead your team through change? Change is hard because it represents the unknown. Your team may not think they need to change. Any time people feel out of control, they become stressed and begin to resist. That is a natural response and the faster you can change the unknown into the known, the better. If your team believes that the price they have to pay outweighs the reward, or if they think the change is not worth the discomfort, good luck—if they do not understand the result or like what they see, they will resist even the most positive change.

You have to be able to clearly answer why the change is happening. Without understanding why a change is being made, emotional ties to the old way of doing things are difficult to loosen. People have to understand why change is necessary before they are willing to let go of the past. Even if they do not agree, they will accept change more rapidly if they understand why the change is occurring.

Grand Entrance

You can help determine your team's enthusiasm for the change by focusing on the entrance of the new while you are working through the exit of the past.

Did you ever walk into a movie only to see the last 10 minutes of the show as the hero and heroine head into the sunset and their life of happiness? All you saw was the outcome. If you were to watch the same movie from the very beginning, your perception would be completely different because you would know what happens in the end. Your stress level would be down, you could relax, and you could enjoy the trials they experience along the way, knowing that, in the end, there will be a storybook ending.

As you lead your people through whatever changes are in the works, keep focused on the result. Visualize and verbalize the positive possibilities your team is about to enter. Talk about the rewards and see change as a leadership challenge. You may be leading your people into the entrance of the greatest time of their career.

Don't be a jerk. Attack complacency.

Don't Be a Jerk
Lead with Confidence

"Something can be done and there is something I can do."
                                                    —Unknown

I am not sure exactly where I heard that sentence for the first time. Whoever shared it with me gave me a wonderful gift—it has been a source of confidence throughout my life. Something can be done—whatever hole I was in was not permanent and something can be done right now. And, there is something I can do—the next move is mine.

Not everything that happens to you is going to be great; you don't live in a Pollyanna world. Things will happen that are beyond your control and maybe unfair and unexplainable. Regardless, you never lose control of your reaction. There are no stipulations. No passes for bad economy, bosses, luck, or choices . . . no stipulations at all. You can react to whatever happens to you in a positive, optimistic, confident manner—or not. Those around you are watching how you react to everything.

What Do You See?

"An optimist sees an opportunity in every calamity; a pessimist sees a calamity in every opportunity." That was Winston Churchill's view. The following story illustrates his point.

Two researchers were independently dispatched by a large shoe manufacturer to one of the world's least-developed countries. The researchers' task was to assess the business possibilities within that country.

When the first report came back to the manufacturer's headquarters, the message read: "No market here. Nobody wears shoes!" A few days later, the second report came back from the other researcher. It read: "Great market here. Nobody wears shoes!" Same country, same situation, but the researchers each viewed things differently.

If you were to conduct a survey and ask, "Are you an optimistic person?" most people would say, "Sure, absolutely. I am optimistic." They may add, "but I am also a realist." Even the first guy in the shoe story above would consider himself an optimist but also a realist. But, like many people do, he fixated on one thing and could not see the greater picture. He was not an optimist or a realist. The second guy in the story looked beyond the obvious and saw something good in the situation and focused on the opportunity. He was an optimist and a realist.

Optimism is a state of mind. It is the result of your desire and effort to make every situation the best possible. It breeds confidence. Certainly, life is not without potholes. Everyone is faced with setbacks and unexplainable events that are unexpected and sometimes destructive. The question is not whether you will face difficult situations—the question is, how do you move forward regardless of the situation?

A confident leader recognizes that defeat is a temporary setback, isolated to a given situation. Unexpected events will happen. You will be shoved onto unfamiliar paths that test you. Regardless of the struggles you are confronting, you can still lead your team with optimism and confidence. How you look at things will ultimately influence what happens down the road.

Attitude Is Internally Controlled

Your attitude impacts every aspect of your life. If you look closely, you'll find that attitude becomes the linchpin for your opportunities, your circumstances, your successes, and your failures. Many people subscribe to the theory that your attitude is simply a reflection of external circumstances; the automatic response to something negative is negative, and the automatic response to something positive is positive. Whatever happens to us dictates how you respond.

I don't buy into that theory. Your attitude is internally controlled. No external situation has control over your own attitude.

Your attitude is powerful. Doctors confirm that the difference between survivors of serious illnesses and those who do not survive is often the attitude of the patient. In sports, coaches will tell you the attitude of the team is as important as the game plan. In school, teachers have found that positive kids produce positive results. People are more productive when they are around positive people.

If positive attitudes make you happier, more productive, and more successful, why would anyone choose negativism—a self-inflicted wound? Why would anyone choose to hurt themselves by being negative?

Successful people choose not to inflict the poison of negative attitudes on themselves. People who are positive and confident attract others like a magnet. Positive and enthusiastic people add energy to those around them, whereas negative and cynical people zap that same energy, draining the room of confidence.

I cannot name one successful person who people would describe as negative and cynical. Not one. Can you? Do you think it is coincidental? I don't think so. Optimism and confidence are two traits that you will find in great leaders, regardless of industry, profession, or age.

A confident, enthusiastic attitude is more important to your success than how you dress, how you look, how much skill you have, how much education you've accumulated, and how gifted you think you are. The good news is that you have an opportunity to choose the attitude you have for each situation every day.

All too often we may want to blame our attitude about something on past events and experiences in our lives. Charles Dickens advised in *A Christmas Carol*, "Reflect upon your present blessings, of which every man has many—not on your past misfortunes, of which all men have some." Don't brood over mistakes, carry grudges, or harbor hate—each of those negative emotions possesses the power to prevent you from success.

A major difference between successful people and others is that successful people insist on reliving and re-creating past success. They find ways to duplicate their success, even though the situation has changed. Those with less success insist on reliving their past failures and wind up duplicating those failures. They allow their past to eat their future.

Look Inside

Your attitude is a magnet. You attract others who have the same attitudes. Consider this story:

A salesman moved into a new town and met an old-timer as he was leaving the bank. "I'm new to your town. What are the people like here?" the salesman asked. "What were the people like in the town you came from?" the old-timer responded. "Well, they were glum and negative and always complaining, and their glasses were always half-empty," the salesman replied.

"Hmmm," said the old-timer. "Sounds about like the people who live here."

A few weeks later, another person moved to the same town and met the same old-timer as he was leaving the same bank. "I'm new to your town. What are the people like here?" the newcomer asked. "What were the people like in the town you came from?" the old-timer responded. "Well, they were wonderful. They worked together in the neighborhood, helped each other out, and were always there to support us during tough times. We're going to miss them," the newcomer replied.

"Hmmm," said the old-timer. "I think you will like it here. That sounds about like the people who live here."

The old-timer's message? If you want to be around people who are positive, enthusiastic, and eager to live life to the full, your attitude has to be the same. If you think the people around you are glum and negative, you probably ought to check yourself. You may be glum and negative, too.

Something Can Be Done . . .

One of the enemies that destroy your confidence is worry. Worry creates anxiety and fear. Worry places you where you have to make a choice: You can dwell on the situation and let anxiety build or you can begin to attack what is causing you to worry.

Being consumed by worry is choking or strangling your positive thoughts and emotions. It is to suffer from disturbing thoughts. Worry drains your energy and obstructs you from seeing positive possibilities. Not much good happens when you are choked with worry—it torments you.

Most of what you worry about is beyond your control to change. A large portion of what you probably worry about is what people will think or say about you. You do not have any control over what they think or say, so why not spend your time doing something they will admire and then let them talk all they want?

Something can be done: You can prevent worry from consuming your thoughts and energy. The antidote to worry is making a decision to proactively do something to prevent what you are worried about from happening.

A famous study[1] estimated that the average person worries about:

- Things that will never happen—40 percent of the time
- Things about the past that can't be changed—30 percent of the time
- Things about criticism by others, mostly untrue—12 percent of the time
- Health, which gets worse with stress—10 percent of the time
- Real problems that can be solved—8 percent of the time

Someone once told me worrying must work, since 40 percent of what we worry about never happens. That is a pretty clever analysis and proves that you make any case you want to with statistics. However, a person consumed by worry cannot confidently lead others.

Many years ago, Dr. Charles Mayo observed that worry not only puts a strain on our mental health, but on our physical health, too. According to Dr. Mayo, "Worry affects the circulation and the whole nervous system. I've never known a man who died from overwork, but I've known many who have died from doubt."[2] Since Mayo's discovery, researchers have connected chronic worry to weakened immune systems, cardiovascular disease, neurological imbalances, clinical depression, and other physical and psychological dysfunctions. So, those who say they are worried sick or worried to death are probably right.

Worry will choke you. Is there anything worse than not being able to take a breath? When you were a kid and had your breath knocked out, was anything more frightening? You were scared almost to death. Don't be choked by life's worries and allow them to consume your confidence and optimism.

Not worrying isn't easy. For most, including me, it is a real struggle. We all have plenty to worry about if we choose—personal problems, financial issues, concerns about our children and parents, and plenty of other things that pop up. But the fact is that worry cannot change the past and worry does not have to control your future.

There Is Something You Can Do . . .

One antidote to worry is to recognize that you are wasting your energy and emotions on something beyond your control that cannot be changed. You can't change the weather or many natural events. However, for those things which are in your control, there is something you can do to attack worry and become a confident leader. Try the following:

- Get the facts. Most worry is based on false assumptions—your assumption about things that you fear will happen as opposed to what is actually happening. Get the real facts, and try not to worry about the unknown fears that drain your energy.
- Consider the worst possible outcome. If your worry is among the small percent over which you have control, what will be the effect if it does come to pass? Once you discover the worst possible outcome, you will often find that it is not as bad as you thought. You can probably live with it, even though you may have to make some changes. Your stress normally comes from not

understanding the worst possible outcome so you can deal with it.

- Begin to improve on the worst possible outcome. Create a plan that will begin purposeful action to ensure that the worst does not happen. It is difficult to worry about things you are working diligently to improve. The antidote to worry is taking action to prevent what you are worrying about from happening.

- Let it go. If you have done everything you can to prevent the worry from happening, have taken steps toward solving the issue, let it go. Your worrying is not helping anyone or anything. In fact, it is probably making you and those around you miserable.

Optimistic Confidence

Confident leadership requires that you continually look for the best in yourself. Being positive about yourself may go against your human nature. If you are like most, you are the most critical of yourself and a large percentage of your inner self-talk is negative. You are probably far more careful of what you say to others than what you say to yourself. Should you treat yourself that way? Of course not. You should talk to yourself just like your best friends would talk to you—they would be encouraging, helpful, kind, and positive.

It is hard to be positive without letting go of what makes you negative. Even when you are stressed to the max, you can be a champion at positive self-talk. It will make a difference in how you feel about yourself and in your ability to have and maintain confident leadership.

Pessimistic confidence. Is that possible? I don't think so. You have to choose to be optimistic or pessimistic, have confidence or not. The choices are not interchangeable. Choose to be an optimistic, confident person instead of a pessimistic person without confidence.

Don't be a jerk. Lead with confidence.

Winning with Class

Leadership is demanding. If you want to lead a great team, you have to be great. If you want great, long-term leadership success you have to win with great class.

The good news is that the rewards for being a great, rather than average, leader are heavily skewed. People want to work for the best, buy from the best, and deal with the best in almost every situation in our society. The best-selling books sell millions more copies than average books. The best movies generate millions more dollars than 50 average movies. Likewise, the rewards for being a great leader are enormous. People flock to winners.

To become great—or continue to be great—you will need more knowledge than you have right now. Someone once advised me that, "The more you learn, the more you earn." At the time, I probably discounted it as an attempt to be clever. But over the years, I've found that was great wisdom.

I have also discovered that learning is contagious. The more I learned, the more people around me wanted to learn. My team's professional growth was a direct correlation to my professional growth.

The joy of leadership is in the gift of knowledge that you give, not in what you receive in return. The purpose of giving is not to receive back in full measure. If you give solely with the expectation of receiving something in return, you are really not giving—you're swapping. If you receive something in return of your gift, what you receive is a bonus—not a repayment of debt.

There are people surrounding you today who could use your experience, advice, and counsel. Just look around . . . people are desperate for help and do not know where to go or who to turn to. You have the experience to make a profound difference in their life just by sharing your knowledge.

What you do with your life will be your legacy. No one requires you to win with class. It is something you do to help someone along the way, to support your colleagues, your friends, and those whom you may not know. It is a gift that comes without a price tag. Your legacy is priceless.

In some cases, you may never know how much you impact the success of others.

Not too long ago, while touring Boston, I passed a cemetery where Ephraim Wales Bull was buried. I had never heard of Ephraim Wales Bull, but the tour guide said he was the person who created Concord grapes. However, he never profited from the grapes because he died before they were marketed in jellies and jams.

The reason I share the story of Ephraim Wales Bull is because the epitaph on his gravestone reads, "He Sowed, Others Reaped." I think that should be our mission as leaders—to keep sowing and allow others to reap. That is what leadership is all about.

The average person has great intentions of making a difference. Intentions do not accomplish anything. The people who find success make the conscious decision to step out and make a difference. I hope you will make that decision.

You could begin today. You could begin right now.

Notes

Introduction

1. Unpublished Saratoga Institute research, 2003.
2. Leigh Branham, *The 7 Hidden Reasons Employees Leave* (New York: Amacom, 2005), 3.
3. This 2011 study was conducted by PDI Ninth House and included data from 2006 to 2010. Some of the results were published in Tom Daniel, "A Long Engagement: How to Retain Top Performers," *Talent Management*, 24.
4. E. Frauenheim, "Managers Don't Matter," *Workforce Management*, April 4, 2010; K. A. Tucker and V. Allman, "Don't Be a Cat-and-Mouse Manager," The Gallup Organization, September 9, 2004, www.brain.gallup.com.

Don't Be Stupid—Coach Smart

1. Justin Kruger and David Dunning, "Unskilled and Unaware of It: How Difficulties in Recognizing One's Own Incompetence Lead to Inflated Self-Assessments." *Journal of Personality and Social Psychology*, 1999.

Don't Be Stupid—Deal with the Sleeping Stars

1. Steve Jobs's Commencement Speech, Stanford University, 2005.

Don't Be Stupid—Synchronize

1. Andy Crowe, *Alpha Project Managers: What the Top 2% Know That Everyone Else Does Not* (Kennesaw, GA: Velociteach, 2006).

Don't Be Stupid—Concentrate

1. Ashton Applewhite, William R. Evans III, and Andrew Frothingham, *And I Quote* (New York: St. Martin's Press, 2003), 241.

Don't Be Stupid—Integrity Counts

1. Michael D. Shear, "Petraeus Quits; Evidence of Affair Was Found by F.B.I.," *New York Times*, November 9, 2012.

2. Jack Welch with Suzy Welch, *Winning* (New York: HarperCollins, 2005), 25.

Don't Be a Jerk—Listen Up

1. M. Lombardo and C. McCauley, "The Dynamics of Management Derailment," Center for Creative Leadership Technical Report #34 (Greensboro, NC: Center for Creative Leadership, 1988).

Don't Be a Jerk—Answer Why

1. Stephen R. Covey, *The 7 Habits of Highly Effective People* (New York: Simon & Schuster, 1989), 30.

Don't Be a Jerk—Encourage

1. Gary P. Guthrie, *1,600 Quotes & Pieces of Wisdom That Just Might Help You Out When You're Stuck in a Moment* (New York: iUniverse, 2003).
2. Louis W. Fry and Melissa Sadler Nisiewicz, *Maximizing the Triple Bottom Line Through Spiritual Leadership* (Stanford, CA: Stanford University Press, 2013), 45.

Don't Be a Jerk—Attack Complacency

1. "A Brief, Early History of Xerox PARC and the Development of the Personal Computer," *High Tech History*, June 2, 2011.

2. "Digital Camera Inventor Explains How Technology Took Down Kodak," *Huffington Post*, May 22, 2013.

3. Scott Peck, *The Road Less Traveled*, 25th Anniversary edition (New York: Touchstone, 2003), 15.

Don't Be a Jerk—Lead with Confidence

1. G. Matthews and A. Wells, University of Cincinnati, 1990.

2. Zig Ziglar, *Christian Post* Guest Columist, December 3, 2009.

Acknowledgments

"Most of the leadership issues we have to address are because of stupid mistakes or the leader acts like a jerk."

Those were words shared several years ago by my friend and colleague, Ken Carnes. Ken is the best executive coach on the planet and we began paying attention—could successful leadership really be so simple? Since then, our observations have confirmed that—although other factors are important—the first two rules of leadership are that simple—don't be stupid and don't be a jerk. Long-term success ultimately depends on making smart decisions based on accurate information and treating others as real people who have dreams, hopes, and desires to do well.

Thank you, Ken, for being by my side in four different organizations. We have enjoyed quite a ride.

Thanks to our CornerStone team, especially to Barbara Bartlett, Melissa Cabana, and Michele Lucia, who all have worked with me for almost 20 years.

Thanks to Matt Holt from Wiley, who accepted my proposal during a five-minute telephone conversation. And to his team who put it all together—Liz Gildea, Shannon Vargo, Deborah Schindlar, and Peter Knox. You have made the production of this book a delight.

And thanks to Lee Colan, Juli Baldwin, Lee Reid, Bill Cattlette, Bob Biddle, Gary Russi, Stephen Williford, and especially my wife, Madeline, for adding some nice seasoning to the book.

Most of all, I'd like to thank God. Thank you for the gift of Jesus and the privilege of sharing with millions of people worldwide encouragement and hope for the future.

Finally, thanks to our 20,000+ CornerStone clients who have been loyal to me. I try to live up to the lessons that you have taught me—Don't be stupid and don't be a jerk.

May God bless you!

About the Author

David Cottrell is president and CEO of CornerStone Leadership. He is a premier authority on leadership and has worked with many of today's most successful organizations, mentoring leaders to peak performance. As a business executive, David has dealt with the obstacles, frustrations, and issues that today's leaders face.

Before founding CornerStone, David held leadership positions with Xerox and FedEx and led the successful turn-around of a Chapter 11 company. An internationally known author, educator, and speaker, he has been a featured expert on public television and has shared his leadership philosophy and lessons with more than 400,000 leaders worldwide.

David has authored more than 25 books, including the perennial best-selling *Monday Morning Leadership*. He is a thought-provoking and electrifying professional speaker, and his powerful wisdom and insights on leadership have made him a highly sought-after keynote speaker.

David can be reached at www.CornerStoneLeadership .com.

Three Ways to Bring
The First Two Rules of Leadership
into Your Organization

1. *The First Two Rules of Leadership* **PowerPoint**^{TM} **Presentation**
   Introduce and reinforce *The First Two Rules of Leadership* to
   your organization with this cost-effective, downloadable
   PowerPoint^{TM} presentation. Includes facilitator guide and
   notes. $99.95

   www.CornerStoneLeadership.com

2. **Keynote Presentation**
   Invite author David Cottrell to
   inspire your team and help
   create greater success for your
   organization. Each presentation
   is designed to set a solid
   foundation for both
   organizational and personal success.

   Contact Michele@CornerStoneLeadership.com.

3. *The First Two Rules of Leadership* **Workshop**
   Facilitated by David Cottrell or a certified CornerStone
   Leadership instructor, this three- or six-hour workshop will
   reinforce the principles of *The First Two Rules of Leadership*. Each
   participant will develop a personal action plan that can make a
   profound difference in their life and career.

   Contact Michele@CornerStoneLeadership.com.

www.**CornerStoneLeadership**.com

Everyone Needs to Lead

Announcing

Leadership **development for every employee** in your organization:

Increase personal accountability
Bridge the Accountability Gap

Navigate and lead change
Engaging in change at every level

Enable employee owned and led performance
Leading the Performance Connection

Establish relationships; move beyond just communication
Cultivating your Sphere of Influence

Accelerate your high potential development
Experiential learning for your top talent

Employee Led

Leader Supported

Organization Enabled

Please click on the Cornerstone Learning logo at www.cornerstoneleadership.com
to develop the leader in every employee!

CornerStone
Leadership Institute

Other Books by David Cottrell

136 Effective Presentation Tips
175 Ways to Get More Done in Less Time
Birdies, Pars, and Bogeys: Leadership Lessons from the Links
Becoming the Obvious Choice
David Cottrell's Collection of Favorite Quotations
Escape from Management Land: A Journey Every Team Wants Their Leader to Take
Indispensable! Becoming the Obvious Choice in Business and in Life
Listen Up, Customer Service
Listen Up, Leader
Listen Up, Teacher
Leadership . . . Biblically Speaking
Leadership Courage: Leadership Strategies for Individual and Organizational Success
Management Insights: Discovering the Truths to Management Success

Available at **www.CornerStoneLeadership.com.**

Index